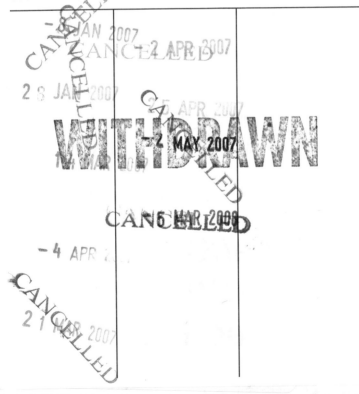

After the Merger

After the Merger

*Seven strategies for successful
post-merger integration*

Max M Habeck

Fritz Kröger

Michael R Träm

FINANCIAL TIMES

Prentice Hall

PEARSON EDUCATION LIMITED

Head Office
Edinburgh Gate
Harlow CM20 2JE
Tel: +44 (0)1279 623623
Fax: +44 (0)1279 431059

London Office:
128 Long Acre, London WC2E 9AN
Tel: +44 (0)20 7447 2000
Fax: +44 (0)20 7240 5771
Website:www.business-minds.com

First published in Great Britain 2000

ISBN 0 273 64354 1

British Library Cataloguing in Publication Data
A CIP catalogue record for this book can be obtained from the British Library.

10 9 8 7 6 5

Typeset by Northern Phototypesetting Co Ltd, Bolton
Printed and bound in Great Britain by Biddles Ltd, Guildford & King's Lynn

The Publishers' policy is to use paper manufactured from sustainable forests.

Contents

About the authors

Max M Habeck

Max M Habeck is Principal and Member of A.T.Kearney's Management Team in Germany. He has worked in the fields of corporate strategy and post-merger integration. From 1995 to 1998, he was a member of A.T.Kearney's Cleveland office and worked with US clients to facilitate their merger efforts.

Fritz Kröger

Fritz Kröger – who holds a PhD in Business Administration – has been working as a management consultant since 1976 in Europe, the USA and Japan. His main expertise is in the field of strategy, restructuring and post-merger integration. As Vice President of A.T.Kearney in Germany, he co-chairs A.T.Kearney's Global Strategy Initiative.

Michael R Träm

Michael R Träm is also Vice President at A.T.Kearney in Germany and his core focus is on strategy and restructuring. He has a PhD in Law and extensive experience in international mergers and acquisitions in various industry projects throughout Europe.

The contributors

Adriane Bergl

Robin Black

Johannes Gerds

Sven Gerlach

Christoph Müser

Dirk Pfannenschmidt

Thomas Rösch

Björn Röper

Robin Young

Acknowledgements

The authors first and foremost are grateful to A.T.Kearney clients as well as all companies around the globe that have gone through at least one merger. Each one has provided us with insight – through the Global PMI survey we did in 1998/99 or through our own project work.

Challenging insight was provided by a number of colleagues who contributed in one way or another to this book. These knowledgeable A.T.Kearney Vice Presidents and Principals are: Jonathan Anscombe, Tim MacDonald and Giorgio Padula. They all made sure that their specific consulting experience was captured by this book. We are indebted to each of them. Further thanks go to Jane Carmichael and Martha Peak, who made sure that this is a global book.

Our book would not be interesting, well-structured and readable if it were not for the guiding input of our project manager Marianne Denk-Helmold, who got the project through to completion by "tugging and tweaking" as needed, and Frank Luby, who provided broad merger knowledge from consulting experience as well as the flavor of American English. Many thanks to both of them.

Foreword

A record number of mergers are making headlines and prompting questions about which will ultimately succeed and which will fail. Although integration is not without stress for an organization and employees, mergers can succeed if companies develop and adhere to a highly disciplined strategy of adding value on day one while implementing a blueprint for future growth.

Since 1992, Tyco International has acquired and integrated more than 110 companies. We gauged these and other potential acquisitions on their ability to expand our core businesses, making sure that their growth potential would be long-term and sustainable.

We have learned that speed is the driver of successful integration, as authors Max M Habeck, Fritz Kröger and Michael R Träm accurately point out. Once discussions have been initiated, we begin making plans for implementation during due diligence. Between the merger announcement and completion dates, we have identified the leaders and developed a one-, two- and three-year plan with them.

At Tyco, we implement the short-term integration plan within weeks, which eliminates uncertainties and shifts the focus to achieving growth for the merged companies. While we justify our acquisitions using the cost savings that can be achieved – and achieved during the first few weeks of integration – we are talking about and seeking ways to generate internal growth from the time we begin due diligence.

The worst mistake is to leave employees without a sense of the goals and objectives of the merger, so communication is vital. Employee understanding and buy-in are particularly necessary to achieve the early-on reductions as well as growth. You can't just eliminate costs without implementing appropriate incentives and direction for growing the company. Likewise, you can't just provide incentives for growth if you're not going to take out the costs. They go hand in hand for successful integration and shareholder value.

Merging companies often get caught up in the details. They must be willing to accept getting 80 percent of it right because integration must happen as quickly as possible. In our experience, you establish the leaders, they take out cost redundancies by consolidating duplicative operations using a best-practices approach, and then you start turning the course for growth, all at the same time.

Incentives that reward employees who are willing to take risks and don't penalize failure also further the goals of integration and growth. Incentive systems for good ideas and prudent risk taking are an important part of our culture at Tyco, the major cultural influence we bring to acquired companies.

After the Merger offers an especially powerful blueprint on how post-merger integration should be done and reflects many of the merger lessons we have learned. Companies with mergers in mind – no matter what their size – would do well to consider these principles *before* signing on the dotted line.

L Dennis Kozlowski
Tyco International

Introduction
Win-win mergers – how it is done

The likelihood that employees will experience at least one merger during their working life has reached an all-time high globally and shows no sign of relenting. The likelihood that this will affect members of top management is growing at an even faster pace. In fact, it is nearly 100 percent certain that within the years to come, a top manager will be involved in a merger or acquisition – either as a target or in the active role of the acquirer.

What many studies say – and just recently a global survey conducted by A.T.Kearney, Management Consultants, has yielded comparable results – is an undisputed truth nowadays: high percentages of all mergers worldwide fail to create value. In some cases they even destroy it.

A brief look into history reveals that the issues of mergers neither creating dividends nor stock price appreciation, as well as the issues involved in trying to remedy this, have been discussed for over 30 years. In spite of the myriad theoretical or practical books on how to make M&A projects really work, the progress on the learning curve seems quite slow. Yet there are always some who do it right the first time. What are they doing right that obviously some others do wrong?

After 20 years of successfully supporting top executives in post-merger integration, we have decided to make our practical experience public. We do believe that companies and managers can do better and we want to give them orientation where needed and foster their self-confidence when they are already on the right track.

If M&A and its aftermath are topics for each and every top manager, the ones who comply with the rules and then speed up and shorten their learning curve will be better prepared for the next challenge than those without this practical support. Making these companies successful in times of economic turmoil is our main objective.

Max M Habeck, Fritz Kröger and Michael R Träm

PART 1

Merger addiction

The rush to create shareholder value

Value creation is the credo. When companies merge the good news gets all the attention: greater efficiency and effectiveness, growth potential, increases in profitability. These great expectations become self-fulfilling prophecies, as the stock market analysts jump on the bandwagon. Companies can't seem to get enough of this rush for shareholder value.

The changing nature of merger activity is almost as dramatic as the headlines. As mergers grab more attention, the total number of mergers worldwide is up nearly 30 percent. In the last five years, the average deal size has more than tripled to above $100 million. This current generation of corporate mergers promises to reconfigure the success model of the past, creating new combinations on a grand scale with increased expectations for long-term market dominance and shareholder returns.

More than 80 percent of companies recently involved in mergers cited "growth" as the leading factor with "achieving cost synergies" a distant second. The chance to reap significant gains from scope and scale opportunities means that more merger managers will need to deftly apply solid integration skills while at the same time operating on an unprecedented scale.

> A global survey of 115 transactions conducted by A.T.Kearney in 1998/1999 revealed that 58 percent of mergers failed to reach the value goals set by top management.

While value creation might be the credo, value destruction is often the fact. A global survey of 115 transactions, conducted by A.T.Kearney in 1998/1999, revealed that 58 percent of mergers failed to reach the value goals set by top management. Instead of taking their companies to the next level, the two partners who joined forces ended up disappointing their constituencies, underperforming their peers, and destroying value in more than half of the cases.

Was there something wrong with the strategies of the companies that did not succeed? Did they just not listen to Peter Drucker, who suggested nearly 20 years ago that a merger should not merely be based on financial expectations but on down-to-earth commonalities such as markets or technology? Did they fail to draw lessons from successful tools like the "pathfinder model" that GE Capital introduced to mergers and acquisitions (M&A) back in the 1980s? That model incorporates "strategy formulation" into the steps to be taken before an acquisition: what are we aiming at? How do we want to reach our goals? In the worst of cases, perhaps some felt that a strategic rationale was secondary for their merger or acquisition, because they succumbed to the persuasive arguments of short-term financial opportunities. We wanted to find out what was happening in those cases where value was being destroyed. Why does all the good advice suddenly go unheeded once the merger is underway and its scope becomes clear in all its complexity? We also wanted to learn from the winners.

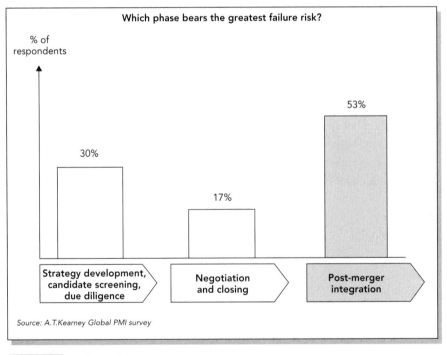

Fig. 1   Failure risks by merger phase

Figure 1 clearly shows that two phases are critical to the success or failure of a merger. Some 30 percent of survey respondents stressed the importance of the pre-merger phase, where the scene is set and preparations are made for implementation. The majority, however, said that the actual implementation phase – the "post-merger integration (PMI)" phase – bears the greatest risks. These responses, combined with other compelling results of our survey, inspired us to explore the merger-integration phase in more depth. The major part of this book is devoted to guidelines to help companies through this crucial phase. But first we would like to examine what goes on when two companies merge, what steps they take successfully before the deal closes, and how these steps influence the PMI phase.

Our intent is to overcome the vagueness of general, well-intended advice and illustrate – case by case and rule by rule – how you can do better when you embark on a merger.

Managing the changes mergers bring

Experience tells us that even though some mergers may be cost-driven and others built on growth expectations, they are always about change. Post-merger integration is most often the key to their success. Change in any environment is a challenge. Your preparation had better be thorough. Management has to understand change, anticipate it, and prepare for as many aspects of change as one can imagine.

M&A is increasingly becoming a more integral part of business life. The idea of a "mega deal" is haunting the top floors of the world's largest companies. Just look around. Two years or so ago, not even the most seasoned analyst would have had the faintest idea of what has recently happened. Monoliths like Deutsche Bank/Bankers Trust and Citigroup are forming the world's largest financial services institutions, while Chrysler and Daimler – two giants of the automotive world – are executing a "merger of equals." Every day new deals are announced, and various stakeholders greet them with reactions ranging from euphoria to skepticism.

When involved in or affected by a merger or an acquisition, people belonging to the buying company initially do not feel much hardship. They belong to the new parent and they feel little reason to anticipate much change. If two roughly equal parties merge, however, change hits both sides. Changes in attitude evolve, slowly but surely. In extreme situations, both companies simply keep on doing what they did separately prior to the deal, but in a less positive frame of mind than before the merger announcement.

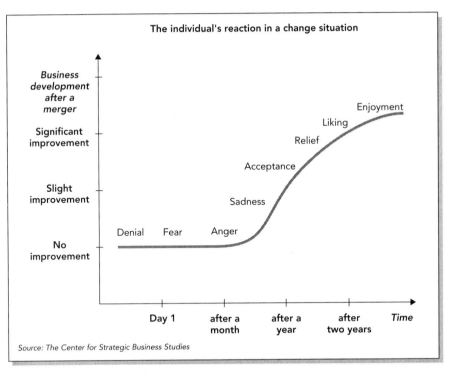

Fig. 2 Behavior during a merger

Why employees react this way has to do with five factors found in any situation where people and change are involved:

■ loss of status and former sphere of influence;

■ lack of transparency about the company's intentions;

■ fierce fight for survival;

■ increased workloads because some people leave, either voluntarily or involuntarily;

■ spillover effect on personal lives.

Growth – thinking big and small at the same time

Companies have to understand that growth does not occur naturally because you add up the sales of two companies that were separate before the merger. Growth is triggered when the right merger partner is found after a careful and thorough search and when the new company does much more than exploit efficiency synergies. The company must be positioned to offer new products, make quantum leaps in engaging new technologies, go after new customers, or even create a new industry. Growth means using your combined resources in such a way that "one plus one makes more than two." If executed properly, mergers can contribute to national, continental and global growth, increasing both the wealth of companies and the living standards of individuals.

> Growth means using your combined resources in such a way that "one plus one makes more than two."

Today's merger managers face a dilemma. They feel the pressure to "think big," but must also be as cost efficient as possible or, in other words, "think small." The way managers currently tackle this paradox often lacks elegance and consistency. A strategy of merely exploiting cost synergies and growing by adding one plus one is an anachronism in today's merger environment. Unfortunately, many merging companies seem to be neglecting the strategic approaches and the corresponding types of mergers to fulfill them.

Different strategies, different merger types with different success expectations

- **Scale.** Gaining clear economies of scale is the strategic rationale and the main economic focus of the acquiring company. These mergers are done mostly in mature industries. They are aimed at reducing unit costs or excess capacity in highly competitive and often deregulated environments such as steel or heavy machinery, banking, or just recently, utilities. Approximately 70 percent of all current mergers fall into this category.

▶

- **Stream.** The strategic intention is vertical integration upstream and/or downstream along the value chain. Few companies have recently merged with this strategy in mind. It has been done, for example, in the oil industry to integrate exploration capability or acquire a retail position.

- **Concentric.** These mergers are done for value enhancement, where an improved value proposition is made to the same group of customers as before the merger. Examples include banks who buy insurance companies and general management consultants who purchase IT services firms.

- **Lateral.** These mergers brought little success in the 1980s. Their main strategic objective is to focus heterogeneous businesses around a central competence. An example would be an automaker trying to branch out into the much broader sector of "technology."

The more successful companies that transact mergers today focus on size, scale and – ultimately – solid growth. Realistic visions and appropriately targeted strategies with clearly defined objectives have taken the place of wishing and hoping. That is the positive message of the A.T.Kearney Global PMI survey. These new, well-thought-out objectives are not the products of merger mania, when whole management teams convince themselves they can generate savings by investing in unrelated companies or industries with cultures and processes quite opposite to their own.

A.T.Kearney's Global PMI survey offers insights into the successful mergers of the 1990s. Those successful companies have done many things right. In detail, they tend to do the following.

- **Rely on experience.** Some 74 percent employed experienced management for the merger tasks.

- **Stay close to home.** The top acquirers have bought related businesses in 80 percent of the cases: 36 percent of acquired companies were in completely-related and 44 percent in highly-related businesses.

■ **Focus on a strong core.** Some 48 percent of companies with the best merger results operate with a strong core business. Only 19 percent of the least successful do so.

■ **Have deep financial resources.** Financial strength makes a significant difference. Those with the most successful mergers had better financial resources than the less successful ones.

■ **Avoid "mergers of equals."** A merger of equals is not a success recipe. Among top performing mergers, only 7 percent were mergers of equals.

So have things really improved in the last 20 years?

We would answer with a qualified "yes." Many recent mergers and acquisitions have been strategic in nature. They were intended to bring about a quantum leap to make the companies more competitive. Given the nonetheless persistent failure rate of mergers, however, we cannot yet give an "all clear" signal.

This positive and less positive news highlights a situation in constant flux. Some key issues have been understood, but some still need to be clarified and improved before mergers can truly become a standard and practical, commonplace strategic tool for corporate development and growth.

What can go wrong will go wrong

There are still several areas in which merging companies fail miserably. Instead of consistently and convincingly doing the essential things right, companies, in the majority of cases, still do them insufficiently, according to our survey and our practical experience. Problems occur regularly in the following areas.

■ **Vision.** Merger partners lack a clear idea of what their merger is up to. What you frequently read about in newspapers and business magazines is that they want to cut costs and/or realize synergies in some respect. Maybe these announcements are made because the stock market rewards these promises in the short term. Tell them you will cut costs in the short term and analysts will like you; tell them you have a vision and a sound strategy for the long-term future of the new entity you want to create, and some analysts will be reluctant to believe you. Rarer are the mergers which stress both aspects and properly emphasize the latter.

- **Leadership.** Companies are not very fast in assigning leadership. A high proportion of them tend to tolerate leadership chaos that eventually degenerates into the survival of the fittest. This wastes precious time and resources, while also causing uncertainty and demotivation among the workforce.

- **Growth.** Organizations do still see growth as an overriding merger rationale, but focus far too much on cost synergies. They get away with a short-term success that will not be sustainable. After whatever sort of cost cutting they might achieve, organizations tend to simply swing back into an accustomed operating mode from before the merger, instead of growing.

- **Early wins.** Companies often lose contact with reality by believing that employees will buy into the merger as soon as it is announced. In fact, almost everyone in both companies will initially feel that the merger will not bring success. In other words, buy-in can never be assumed. It must be earned. If early wins – quick, positive, tangible results – can be created and communicated appropriately, people will begin to acknowledge that there is indeed a brighter future for them and their company.

- **Culture.** Companies all too often decline to acknowledge that cultural barriers exist and that they cannot be removed quickly. They neglect the fact that change must happen and must therefore be addressed in a professional manner.

- **Communication.** Many companies have communication managers in place, professionals whose aim is to improve and smoothen the transfer from two companies into one. What they do not have is the right form of communication. This task requires not just newsletters to employees and well-formulated letters to customers, but also active involvement which – to a large extent – will diminish the uncertainty and frustration of staff. This contributes to a sense of fair play and openness.

- **Risk management.** Companies poorly manage the various risks that are part of any merger situation. Risks are hardly ever talked about. If risks are discussed at all, they are not managed properly, which is why they soon become threats, barriers or even disasters. More care with risk management could change that picture.

Setting the stage for post-merger integration *before* the deal closes

What can companies involved in a merger or acquisition do to prevent the hangovers that strike the majority of mergers? They need to manage their post-merger integration more consciously and professionally. To help this process the companies can take several steps before their deal closes and the post-merger integration phase begins. First, they must perform comprehensive due diligence in the pre-merger phase. By comprehensive, we mean extending the traditional financial due diligence to encompass strategic and business issues.

Financial due diligence focuses on a target's past. But acquirers nowadays have to be much more future-oriented. This demands a due diligence that integrates business issues such as customers, competitors and costs, to support the growth behind the merger.

In order to proceed, the combined companies need a common direction. A deal will succeed when competitive advantages can be created or enhanced leading to growth. Without the accompanying assessment of the overall strategy and its operational implications in sales and marketing, the financial due diligence is limited in its usefulness. Backed up by a more strategy-oriented due diligence, the post-merger integration phase can begin on much firmer ground.

We have also experienced, again and again, that a joint program office which continues the "war room" used during the due diligence is an essential component of successful mergers. Established before the deal closes, it often becomes the physical manifestation of the integration process, the hub of the overall activity, the eye of the hurricane.

■ A program office ensures that guiding principles and general strategy outline by top management are translated into measurable targets and executable tasks. Later on it monitors progress, highlights potential problems, and co-ordinates change management.

■ High caliber individuals from both companies should view the program office as their first common experience and should jointly undertake the support, monitoring and control functions to push merger activities.

- Because of its unique position and intelligent bilateral staffing, a program office can help defuse many of the issues that might otherwise impede progress.

This may sound very basic. But, in our experience, companies frequently neglect to take enough care to organize themselves in this way.

What successful post-merger integration boils down to

The seven rules of merger success are not rocket science. They recognize that three areas of action are crucial during the post-merger integration process.

- **Buy-in.** There has to be buy-in from all levels of management and employees. This must be achieved early and quickly.

- **Orientation.** People have to be well-informed and oriented in order to support the vision and merger rationale. The new company needs a clear compass – an overall direction from day one onward.

- **Expectations.** All expectations – inside and outside the merging companies – must be managed in a proactive and direct way. This means open and honest information up front, then ongoing communication throughout the post-merger integration process.

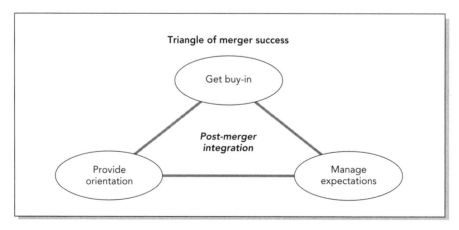

 **Fig. 3** Three focal points of PMI

None of the seven rules that follow represents a self-contained recipe for successful post-merger integration. There is no single, simple Holy Grail for this kind of work. But by following the guidelines in the next chapters in an orchestrated way, you can be sure of having the best chance of effectively integrating the merging companies, realizing your strategy and creating long-term shareholder value.

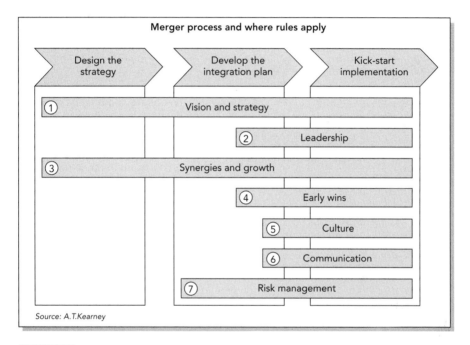

Fig. 4 Merger process overview

PART 2

The seven rules of merger success

Rules that must be applied regardless of the objective

Vision

Create a clear vision and strategy –
you have to deliver

Summary

At first glance, post-merger integration presents a seemingly insurmountable list of tasks to accomplish. The partners need to learn about each other and learn to live with each other. There are a host of business due diligence issues to be examined, opportunities to explore, and decisions to make regarding the allocation of the company's combined resources. But, first and foremost, vision is important.

In our Global PMI survey, we discovered two key facts that will help you understand the importance of vision.

✳ **Fact one: fit is first, not vision.**
Some 78 percent of mergers are mistakenly driven by fit, not vision.

✳ **Fact two: the majority of mergers fail.**
More than half of all mergers – around 58 percent – ultimately fail.

Vision is the only true acid test to determine whether you are on the right track as you prioritize, execute and interpret your post-merger integration tasks. The tough lesson for merging companies to learn is that fit flows from vision, not the other way around.

You have a feeling of exhilaration because you are finally putting your strategy of "growth by acquisition" into practice. After an exhaustive search, you and your team have found the ideal merger partner for your company, which manufactures a wide range of products for industrial and consumer use.

You have made the agreement public, and cannot wait to begin looking at the details and realizing the dream of growth the merger promises.

One evening you meet an old business school friend for dinner. Your friend works as an analyst and covers your industry for a large investment bank. As you enter an elevator on the way to the restaurant, your friend mentions that the merger has been in all the newspapers and that you have appeared on TV at least three times that afternoon alone. Then comes the question you have been eagerly waiting for:

"So … what's your vision?"

Great question! And you have the great answer to go with it.

You begin by listing a whole series of marketing initiatives you want to undertake, then hint at some new product development ideas your merger partner has had sitting in a drawer for, believe it or not, years. You tell your friend that electronic commerce is not the wave of the future, it is the wave of right now, and you plan to capitalize on opportunities there. Then there is India. Maybe you could move all your data processing to a company in Bangalore to save costs and use the comparative advantage of Indian software programmers in this area. Between that and a production site in southern China, you will be able to compete globally.

"So what do you think?" you ask, as the elevator indicates you have reached your desired floor. But the answer and general reaction of your friend do not meet your expectations.

"Did you know that this elevator is supposed to hold 11 people?" your friend asks nonchalantly. "Where would they all fit?"

Many aspects of running a business – from strategy to goals to plans – can easily be mistaken for vision. But the development of proper vision, as we describe in this section, has become more important than ever as the pace of change in global business continues to accelerate. In the case of change brought about by a merger, the vision for the combined company forms the touchstone in your efforts to gain buy-in and to set and manage clear expectations. Above all, it provides the orientation which is crucial to harnessing and focusing your company's resources.

The technology and events which drive today's business world were nothing more than political or science fiction just ten years ago. No one cared about buzzwords like "convergence" in the 1980s. No one thought about how information systems would become part of strategic decisions. Even "prophets" like Alvin Toffler or John Naisbitt did not foresee the turmoil which currently reigns.

CEOs feel they have lost some control. They also feel overwhelmed by the revolutionary change which has become – as often cited by Bob Kidder from the US food products company Borden – a regular feature of the global business policy environment.

Opportunities in emerging and post-communist markets as well as established markets have hastened the trend toward globalization. The strengthening of bonds among the members of trading blocs and talk groups from Mercosur to ASEAN has sparked a wave of privatization. Governments have responded to free market pressure by throwing the markets of their national champions wide open. Subsidies, meanwhile, dwindle or disappear.

> The number of companies worldwide is diminishing every day in the banking, insurance and automotive industries, just to name a few.

Examples of revolutionary change and "cannot control" feelings of CEOs are widespread: the number of companies worldwide is diminishing every day in the banking, insurance and automotive industries, just to name a few. At the same time, visionaries build entirely new industries, which generate tremendous growth and raise living standards.

Over 25 years ago, Intel's Gordon Moore claimed that the engineers at his small Californian company were the true revolutionaries of the 1960s. His law – which says the power of computer chips will double around every 18 months – spurred the development of one backbone of the PC industry, which grew into a roughly $150-billion-per-year global business in just 20 years.

Without chips from Intel, software from Microsoft, routers from Cisco Systems, and access provided by America Online, wouldn't we feel catapulted back to the Stone Age? Would we still be able to carry out our business processes, from R&D to invoicing, without their products and services? Or without another now mighty software firm called SAP? And how do we deal with this dependence? How do companies come to terms with today's environment?

Vision lets you withstand change and capitalize on it

A sense of direction – drawn from a clear and realistic vision – has emerged as the last stronghold in this changing business world. The sense of direction enables you not only to withstand the effects of change, but also to confidently initiate change and capitalize on your opportunities. Fortunately, companies have begun to understand this. When everybody and everything, including the targets you set, are in constant motion, you have to maintain an overview and perspective which reflects what your ultimate sense of purpose is.

> Establishing a clear vision is a must to ensure a successful post-merger integration.

Without the strong sense of direction provided by a vision, do you really want to take on the challenge of integrating two different organizations which are facing abrupt change following a merger or acquisition? Establishing a clear vision is a must to ensure a successful post-merger integration. Nonetheless, far too many mergers are attempted without such a clear and realistic vision, no matter what you might read in the press or see on television.

Common business sense, of course, says that you should never pursue mergers and acquisitions without a clear vision and a clear strategy. When an acquiring company's top management attempts to explain and justify a proposed deal to constituencies, they will, of course, claim that these visions and strategies exist. In their proxy statements, press releases, and interviews on CNN, they will reiterate the point: the strategies and vision are clear, and they are being followed.

In the reality of most merger environments, however, you will experience something different. The meaningful idea of a clear vision and an appropriate strategy usually disappears before the deal is done, because a finance-oriented way of thinking tends to predominate.

We all know about the confusion surrounding words such as "vision" and "strategy", along with that impish word which appears in every newspaper or magazine article on a merger or acquisition: "fit."

Using examples from the current merger wave as well as from previous ones, we will first show that poor vision or lack of vision can help bring down a merger. We will then demonstrate that fit – either as financial fit, back-of-the-envelope fit, or ego fit – does not represent an adequate rationale for a merger. Finally, we will offer some guidelines for coming to terms with "vision," including how a broader business due diligence provides you with the factual basis to develop your vision, and what criteria your vision must fulfill.

When you look closely, the news slowly emerging in our globalizing, consolidating, borderless, virtual world is not the long-anticipated collapse into chaos, as captured in ugly words such as hypercompetition. Instead, the news is revealing the seeds of a renaissance of vision, leading to sound, basic strategy as a way of coping, adjusting, then ultimately growing.

The following facts are clear. They are also well-known. Taken together, they become alarming.

✳ **Fact one: fit is first, not vision.**

Our Global PMI survey revealed that 78 percent of all merger transactions are arranged and consummated because someone determined that some kind of "fit" existed. "Fit" frequently focuses on superficial comparisons of customer bases, product lines, or geographic coverage. In other cases, "fit" centers around financial data. The latter case makes some sense, of course,

> Neither superficial fit nor financial fit is the basis for a forward-looking business case.

when you consider that no merger is likely to take place without the completion of an accounting-based due diligence study. A set of thoroughly crunched and cross-checked numbers is necessary to gain everything from analysts' goodwill to stakeholder buy-in to approval from anti-trust authorities.

Neither superficial fit nor financial fit, however, is the basis for a forward-looking business case.

✳ **Fact two: the majority of mergers fail.**

As confirmed by our study of 115 companies worldwide, the majority of all mergers – some 58 percent – ultimately fail.

Some mergers merely fall short of reaching the high expectations set by boards and top management in the euphoria prior to signing the deal. Others may fulfill some expectations, but lag behind their competitors in terms of growth and returns to shareholders. But many of the failures actually destroy value. We say that our study "confirmed" that most mergers fail, because we have yet to see a professional study anywhere by anybody which didn't show that at least half of all mergers don't work. How the success rates break down by merger type is shown in Fig. 5.

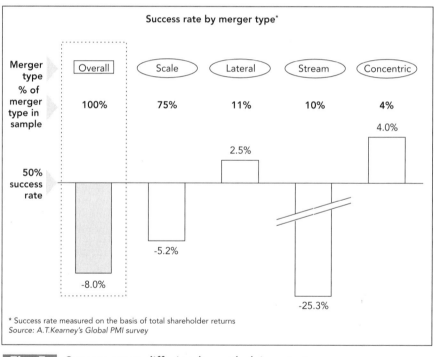

Fig. 5 Success rates differing by underlying strategy

When you combine 78 percent for fit from fact one with the 58 percent failure rate from fact two, it does not take a lot of computing power to figure out that "fit" is not all it's cracked up to be.

Vision means balancing dreams and reality

The creation of a vision is not as simple as it seems at first glance. A merger undertaken with an unclear or unrealistic vision can be just as destructive to shareholder value as a merger based entirely on "fit." Many of these poorer visions have the character of great ideas spawned in late-night discussions. They sound like world beaters at the time, but then most of them wilt under the scrutiny of daylight and clear, sober minds.

This myopia is nothing new. Back in the 1960s – when conglomeration was fueling a merger and acquisition wave and diversification was "in" – the visionaries running two formerly great US companies undertook a promising and ambitious merger which bucked that diversification trend. The deal, in fact, would fit quite nicely into today's merger environment.

The Pennsylvania Railroad and the New York Central Railroad merged in 1968 to form Penn Central, then the largest corporate merger ever in US history. Penn Central shows clearly that the issues and dangers you face today in post-merger integration are nothing new.

Penn Central marked the first great, modern "mega-merger." It was also the first big mega-flop. Its bankruptcy helped wipe an entire industry from the US business landscape. The piles of debt it left in its wake – albeit indirectly – helped launch the career of Michael Milken.

Penn Central

After six years of negotiation and regulatory red tape, the US railroads Pennsylvania and New York Central finally merged in 1968. The merger seemed set to realize the vision of a seamless passenger and freight service along the east coast of the United States. The newly-formed company had assets valued at $6.3 billion and annual sales of around $2 billion.

These two companies had a special place in the hearts of Americans. The Pennsylvania is immortalized with its own space on the Monopoly game board, while the New York Central – with its Grand Central Station – was built up by one of the original industrial barons, Cornelius Vanderbilt.

Penn Central was losing an estimated $1 million per day when it filed for bankruptcy on 23 June 1970. The reasons cited for the merger's failure include poor morale, incompatible computer systems and signals, poor maintenance, low customer demand, unreliable service, an unmanageable debt burden, a national liquidity crunch, regulatory interference and congressional indifference. Given this range of problems, it seems that the original vision of a seamless rail service in the eastern United States – no matter how clear it seemed and how good it sounded – was simply unrealistic under the prevailing circumstances.

Penn Central's rapid decline paralyzed rail services in parts of the United States. The infrastructure it left behind did not fully recover until Conrail, the freight service descendant, left government receivership in the 1980s. Penn Central's passenger service, meanwhile, remains part of Amtrak.

Visions that first seemed clear have launched many other merger misadventures. No one should conduct a discussion about the danger of pie-in-the-sky visions without mentioning the bold acquisitions which the German industrial giant Daimler-Benz once made in pursuit of a "worldwide technology corporation." That was then Chairman Edzard Reuter's dream and vision, and he spent over $8 billion on an acquisition spree in the 1980s. This splurge eventually forced Daimler-Benz to undergo a painful restructuring which resulted in the achievement of a world record which Edzard Reuter and his predecessors never dreamed his company would set: the largest financial loss in a single year by a German company.

In a similar vein, AT&T had what seemed like a convincing vision when it embarked on absorbing the computer company NCR in the early 1990s.

AT&T and NCR

In the late 1980s, American Telephone and Telegraph still had assets such as Bell Labs to go with the long-distance telephone services it kept after the 1984 anti-trust break-up. The company also had a grand vision of a technological synergy between its expertise in telecommunications and NCR's expertise in computer technology, especially in the open systems which NCR sold successfully in the banking and retailing sectors.

NCR, formerly known as National Cash Register, had made a successful transition to the computer world and had a $6 billion business when AT&T came calling in what was initially perceived by NCR as a hostile takeover.

After years of intense searching – hampered by management changes as well as cultural friction – no synergies were found. The presumed fit between telecommunications equipment and computer hardware failed to turn up.

AT&T spun off the remains of NCR around five years later at a loss of around $3.5 billion, nearly half of what it initially paid.

AT&T can be found at **www.att.com**

Examples from companies around the globe gave us the explicit idea that in today's rapidly changing and consolidating business world, following an unrealistic vision or putting "fit" first will leave you with the lowest chances of laying the foundation for a successful merger. "Fit" is obviously often used as a rationale, however, when there is nothing else to put forward.

The "fit" fetish needs to be debunked

Fitting one company with another has many aspects. But there is a big difference between the fit which an investment banker legitimately sees – which by definition will be financial – and the fit which a management consultant understands when two companies fit together well from a strategic perspective.

Many of those involved in a merger – from managers to investment bankers – seem to have a fetish with the word "fit." Based on our survey results, we have been able to identify three forms of "fit," none of which seem on their own to be a plausible reason to spend billions of dollars to acquire a company. Each one fails because it is neither broad enough nor deep enough to provide direction to the new company and drive post-merger integration forward. These fit forms are:

- financial
- back-of-the-envelope
- ego.

Financial fit ignores many "hard" and "soft" factors

In the 1980s, many of the mergers and acquisitions were not about people and how they could work together. They were clearly about eliminating them, especially those who were supposedly mismanaging their companies.

In those days the paradigm was a triangle connecting cash flow, net present value (NPV), and junk bonds. If you felt that the net present value of your proposed investment in a company was positive, then you would buy. If the resulting cash flow were higher than the amount of service on your junk bonds, did it really matter how leveraged you became?

The new culture of "make money or else" swiftly turned established cultures upside down. It also produced many success stories. Long languishing companies such as Walt Disney were turned into virtual cash machines. Companies with new technologies such as McCaw Cellular received the venture backing they may not have received ten years earlier.

But the often impersonal, ruthless raiders of this era generally treated companies as cash-flow-generating black boxes, and damn the consequences.

Meanwhile, the buyout specialists of firms such as Kohlberg Kravis Roberts (KKR) and Mercury Asset Management placed companies under the Damocles Sword of high leverage, and tied the financial future of executives and managers to the creation of shareholder value. The underperforming companies bought by these firms needed to restructure thoroughly and quickly in order to generate the cash to service and reduce the load of debt they carried.

"Financial fit" was what counted in this world. The other "hard" and "soft" factors discussed in this book were secondary, if they were acknowledged at all.

But the world which those deals shook up is history. The raiders and "barbarians" of the 1980s were very thorough in their efforts to ravage the large herds of underperforming companies which used to roam the business landscape, especially in the US and the UK.

Today's mergers are under a different sort of success pressure. They must be growth-oriented. They need to look at many more factors, both "hard" and "soft", to make gains and be successful.

Back-of-the-envelope fit oversimplifies the underlying issues

A back-of-the-envelope fit is often cited as the rationale for a stream or vaguely scale-based merger. In its best – but very rare – form, it is an elegant solution to rationalizing or enhancing a value chain.

In its more common and worst form, it grossly oversimplifies two complex business areas and then tries to build a seamless link between them. Just take two industries, put them inside little bubbles, then draw an arrow between them, and *voilà*, a great idea is born. Companies immediately begin reaching for their checkbooks.

This method works well in an MBA class, where nobody's money is on the line and we'll never know if everybody lives happily ever after. Unfortunately, it is attempted far too often in the real world as well.

Back-of-the-envelope mergers tend to occur with above-average frequency in the computer and electronics industries. In the last 20 years, no two concepts have been easier to put in bubbles and connect with arrows than hardware and software. These stream mergers seemed to make a lot of sense.

Mergers which have more of a scale orientation have had their victims as well. The benefits of a scale or horizontal merger usually come from direct product similarities, such as when a company buys a direct competitor in order to increase market share. Instead of software/hardware this would mean hardware/hardware. Both look perfect on the back of the envelope.

> Back-of-the-envelope mergers tend to occur with above-average frequency in the computer and electronics industries.

In the special case of a concentric merger, the acquirer seeks to integrate related products into its range, perhaps because the end customers are largely the same or the distribution channels are identical.

So putting two computer hardware companies together seems an easy task without much risk attached. But take a look at what can happen once such a merger leaves the back of the envelope.

Siemens-Nixdorf Informationssysteme

When the German postwar entrepreneur Heinz Nixdorf passed away in 1986, the computer company he had shaped began to struggle. Soon after, the German electronics and engineering giant Siemens AG came in as "white knight" to help rescue Nixdorf. Siemens formed Siemens-Nixdorf Informationssysteme AG (SNI) to combine the two companies' complementary computer lines.

Back in those years, the management at neither Siemens nor Nixdorf nor the newly-formed SNI had a clear and realistic vision about how to make the merger work and what precise strategy the new company should pursue. Their challenge to make SNI work and grow was made harder because the anticipated benefit of the hardware fit – a complete, unified product range – did not materialize.

In 1998 Siemens launched an internal restructuring to integrate the lion's share of SNI into Siemens AG, even though the separate legal unit Siemens Nixdorf continues to be responsible for the point-of-sale systems and self-service product businesses.

Siemens can be found in English at **www.siemens.de/en.com**

Granted, all computers have a central processing unit and therefore have some degree of similarity. But to argue that there are automatic synergies across hardware lines is like saying that heavy trucks and diesel locomotives have much in common because they both have more than four wheels. Siemens Nixdorf came to realize this much too late.

Hardware and software can be combined just as easily on the back of the envelope as hardware and hardware. The purchase of Columbia Pictures by Sony illustrates how a merger can fail, partly because the integration of the two companies never got much beyond the idea of "fit."

Sony Pictures

The vision of wedding consumer electronics (hardware) with motion pictures (software) helped inspire Sony to acquire Columbia Pictures for approximately $5 billion in 1989. Sony's Japanese management then took a hands-off approach to Hollywood and entrusted Columbia's operation to producers Peter Guber and Jon Peters, who came from a small production company Sony had also acquired.

Whether synergies ever existed between the hardware and software quickly became a moot point. Columbia had difficulties generating the successful software to begin with. Rapidly rising salaries for stars and a lack of success at the box office culminated in Sony's making an abrupt accounting change in mid-1994. The company wrote off $2.7 billion and reported additional operating losses of around $500 million in the fiscal year ending 31 March 1995. These losses were attributed to the abandonment of a large number of projects and the settlement of outstanding lawsuits.

Instead of divesting the unit, Sony made management changes and imposed stricter controls. Columbia is now a part of Sony Pictures Entertainment, which represented just under 10 percent of the Sony group's worldwide sales of around $50 billion in 1998.

Sony Pictures Entertainment can be found at **www.spe.sony.com**

Ego fit places the focus on the wrong issues

Mergers involving an ego fit tend to have a "wave the magic wand" quality to them. Sometimes a chief executive wants to leave his mark on a company, or enjoys the sport of the deal-making. Other managers apparently have the goal of putting together the *first, biggest, largest* in an industry, as if the superlative alone was all that matters. And some ego fit mergers are literally real-life back-of-the-envelope deals, where the first announcements are made a matter of days after some sketches were made on some scrap paper.

What is the lesson of a fit's failure when, instead of a rationale, "ego" is the central topic? This simplistic approach to "fit" reveals the three major drawbacks in the "concept" itself.

■ **Fit oversimplifies.** Like the bubbles in the back-of-the-envelope scenario, fit oversimplifies. Fit often delivers little more than a soundbite which turns out to be hollow, once the hard work begins. There may be cases where overcomplexity can and should be met by simplicity. For a merger this does not hold true, because two companies do not harmonize automatically.

■ **Fit says nothing about growth.** Fit soundbites rarely say anything about growth. They describe a historical situation, or at best the status quo, without saying where the company is supposed to be heading, how much it will grow, and how it will achieve that growth. In the extreme cases of financial fit, growth is not even an immediate concern. Cost savings are the reason for the deal.

■ **Fit matters only when clear vision and sound strategy are in place.** The core of the problem with fit lies in the fact that fit does not automatically mean that a clear and realistic vision exists. Nor does it allow you to derive a strategy. It is based on a limited form of analysis which does not capture the business issues central to growing the company. Fit can – and should – only be determined after a vision and a strategy are in place to provide the proper guidance.

> Fit can – and should – only be determined after a vision and a strategy are in place to provide the proper guidance.

We have seen that having a poor vision or placing too much emphasis on fit have sidetracked or even doomed the process of post-merger integration. Companies considering a merger should forget "fit" at the outset, and focus instead on an implementable strategy derived from a clear and realistic vision. The "fit" will then follow.

The definition of a bold "one business vision" is absolutely crucial for a successful transformation. Without a clearly expressed and guiding vision, the transformation effort can easily dissolve into numerous incompatible projects that can take the organization in the wrong direction. In contrast, a "one business" vision provides clear guidelines for reconciling conflicts and reaching decisions in the transition period – for managers at all levels throughout both companies.

The ambitious, uplifting vision the merged companies require should provide more than the general principles of how the new company will operate and compete. It should be extended to derive aggressive financial and operational targets and to incorporate a clearly defined blueprint of the start-up structure.

The main point to keep in mind in constructing such a vision is realism. Is this vision achievable? Does it have the buy-in from employees? Is it based on limit-free thinking? Does it have staying power? Does it provide a clear orientation for the company? Is it backed by the top management? Is it credible, appealing, possible, understandable, straightforward and attractive? And finally, does it make economic sense?

What does my merger partner bring to the table?

You can develop a realistic vision if and only if you perform an honest, objective analysis of what you want to do, and what you and your merger partner are capable of accomplishing in terms of core competencies and financial resources. One important step is to expand the due diligence efforts to include much more than the financial groundwork.

Traditionally, due diligence has been largely limited to financial aspects and is therefore focused on a target's past. At great length, income statements and balance sheets have been analyzed, explaining in great detail why the target's gross margin in the 1992–96 period dropped two percentage points, or why inventory days-on-hand increased from 27 days to 38 over the course of the last 24 months. While this may be intellectually intriguing and stimulating from a financial analyst's point of view, it is fairly irrelevant from a business point of view.

The question which should excite an acquirer the most is: "In the future, what can I offer and what can this target company realistically offer?" This involves examining five areas in detail: customers, capabilities, competitors, costs, and culture. While examining these areas, a good measure of business sense should be brought into play.

Newspapers are currently full of stories about companies looking for partners. The urgent question, however, is not who should team up with whom, but why any company should team up at all. What do you want to gain from a merger? This question must be resolved, regardless of whether you want to buy, get bought, or pool your assets with another company.

The current merger and acquisition wave among high-tech and telecommunications companies exemplifies how fit can flow from vision. Companies ranging from relatively young upstarts such as Cisco Systems and 3Com to 100-year-old giants such as AT&T have either created entirely new industries and markets in the last five years, or are making proactive efforts to influence them.

It has become a cliché to say that the Internet is changing the way everyone lives and works. Early critics of "surfing" dismissed the Internet as a toy or called it the CB-radio of the 1990s. But the following facts illustrate just how much money is at stake in this market.

■ By some estimates, the majority of telecommunications now involves data, not voice. Data transmission is growing at a rate of around 30 percent per year, and e-mails currently outnumber regular mail by a factor of ten on a volume basis.

■ The Internet has reached 50 million people in just four years. Television needed 13 years to do so, and radio needed 35.

■ Cisco Systems, founded in 1984, reached $100 billion in market capitalization faster than any other company in history. Its products form the backbone of Internet transmission networks. Cisco has acquired 25 companies since its founding.

■ 3Com, a competitor of Cisco, has seen its market capitalization grow 40-fold since 1992 to $17.2 billion at the beginning of 1999. 3Com itself has made 19 acquisitions since 1987.

Such companies have given thought to their competitive environment, its future direction, and how they and their merger partners can play a role in it. They show that fit flows from vision and strategy, not the other way around.

Many companies have fortunately begun to realize the significance of vision, from which you derive strategies, set goals, and appreciate your fit with the company you seek to acquire. Because these companies have their vision in place and strategy formulated, they know what they are looking for. And because they know, they rarely encounter problems by teaming up with the wrong partner.

Earlier in this section we mentioned AT&T's attempt to capture technology or product-based synergies by buying computer maker NCR. The new vision which is moving AT&T forward under new CEO Michael Armstrong is strongly customer-focused. AT&T knows that US customers alone are spending over $80 billion a year on voice, video, and other forms of telecommunication. Despite its strong franchise in long-distance telephone service, AT&T receives much less than half of that rapidly growing pie.

AT&T

In case you are still wondering what the historic dimensions of the so-called Digital Age are, take a look at what American Telephone and Telegraph (AT&T) has done since Michael Armstrong took over as CEO in 1997. Armstrong is currently undertaking what might be – at least in dollar terms – the greatest risk in the history of corporate America. In just over a year he has committed to mergers and acquisitions valued at an estimated $140 billion, the equivalent of half the US defense budget and enough money to build approximately 7,000 miles of interstate superhighway – the traditional asphalt kind – from scratch.

What does he want? Customers and high-speed communication lines.

AT&T spent $62.5 billion to buy MediaOne and its 5 million cable TV customers, after having spent $55 billion to acquire TCI and its 11 million customers and high-speed lines. AT&T's vision is to offer these customers – and its current base of long-distance telephone customers – a one-stop shop for all telecommunications needs. These encompass fixed-line and cellular telephony as well as video and high-speed data, all at a bundled discount.

Armstrong, a veteran of IBM and Hughes, feels that AT&T can integrate these companies and still execute its day-to-day business. In summer 1999, the market appeared to agree. AT&T's share price had almost doubled from its low of $32.25 in September 1998, and Microsoft invested $5 billion after expanding a co-operation deal with the company in May. Performance has been strong as well, as AT&T beat analysts' expectations with a revenue increase of 9.9 percent to $14.1 billion in the first quarter of 1999.

AT&T can be found at **www.att.com**

Not to be outdone, US-based MCI – which was originally created over 20 years ago with the vision of a telecom world without the mighty AT&T monopoly – is now part of a global telecommunications company with annual revenues of over $30 billion.

MCI WorldCom

After seeing what AT&T bought for $140 billion, it might be hard to imagine what assets the company does not have. That's where the vision of MCI WorldCom comes in. WorldCom outbid British Telecom for MCI by offering $37 billion for the company in late 1997.

The new firm wants to establish itself as the leading supplier of "local-global-local" connections for data, Internet, and local and international voice communications. The company expects data's share of telecommunications traffic to rise to 95 percent within five years, with much of it travelling on the international backbone the company has assembled.

Due to a lengthy regulatory approval process, the merger was not officially completed until September 1998. The time was used, however, to develop integration plans. The combined company has annual revenues of more than $30 billion and operates in 65 countries.

Realizing a vision is nothing new for MCI, which was founded with the vision of breaking AT&T's telephone monopoly in the US market and then competing with it head-to-head. It succeeded on both counts.

MCI WorldCom can be found at **www.wcom.com**

These customer-driven visions, meant to change the world, have one thing in common: the idea of one-stop-shopping. Whether they will succeed is hard to say, based on evidence from other sectors. Companies in the general retail sector, for example, have had mixed success with the notion than you can offer your customers everything they need in one location. On the one hand, Wal-Mart is rapidly becoming a major food retailer and recently overtook Toys R Us as the top seller of toys and games in the United States. Sears, Roebuck, on the other hand, once thought that the same customer group which buys wrenches and washing machines would also buy stocks and insurance. It has since divested its Allstate and Dean Witter units.

Citigroup, the product of the 1998 merger between Travelers and Citibank, is putting the idea of one-stop-shopping to the test on a global basis in the area of financial services. Travelers has long pursued the idea of becoming a financial supermarket, and the merger with Citibank brings this goal much closer to realization.

Citigroup

US-based Travelers Group has long held the vision of offering its customers access to a supermarket for financial services. Its efforts to assemble Citigroup, the current colossus for global one-stop-shopping in financial services, involved mergers and acquisitions valued at $80 billion within a 12-month period in 1997 and 1998.

These moves included $9 billion for Salomon Inc, $1 billion for a stake in Japan's Nikko Securities, and $70 billion for Citibank. Citibank Chairman John Reed and Travelers Chairman Sanford Weill now serve together as co-CEOs of Citigroup. They face the task of integrating these diverse parts into a single global business which can offer not only standard banking services, consumer lending, credit cards, and asset management, but also life, auto and home insurance.

Reed and Weill face the inevitable culture clashes and turf wars which result when two organizations of this scale merge. But they intend to keep their focus on two areas: taking advantage of cross-selling opportunities and reducing costs.

Citigroup's share price has risen by over 150 percent since its low of $19.00 shortly after the merger was completed in October 1998. This gives the group a market capitalization of around $160 billion. In the second quarter of 1999, the company earned $2.5 billion on revenues of $15.0 billion, exceeding market expectations. At this pace, Citigroup could earn more in 1999 than either General Electric, Microsoft, IBM or General Motors.

The acquisition trend continues as well. In March 1999 the company paid $1.1 billion for the credit card operations of Mellon Bank.

Citigroup can be found at **www.citi.com**

Clear visions and massive markets are not the private domain of high-tech companies or modern financial services companies. The same guidelines and the same needs apply to traditional manufacturing areas as well, such as automobiles. Another example of how a clear vision manifests itself in the choice of a merger partner is the purchase of part of Sweden's AB Volvo by the US automaker Ford Motor Company.

Ford is starting to see its visionary Ford 2000 plan bear fruit. Through the implementation of this plan over the last few years, Ford has come to realize that its focus should be on building cars and light trucks. For this reason, it has recently sold its heavy trucks business to US-based Freightliner, and decided to make the well-publicized purchase of AB Volvo's car division.

Ford Motor

Ford's purchase of AB Volvo's automotive division for $6.45 billion at the beginning of 1999 shows the US automaker is really sticking to its stated vision for the 21st century, namely, "to become the world's leading consumer company that provides automotive products and services."

This is not the kind of wide-eyed transportation vision which might have compelled Ford to swallow Volvo whole, thereby also acquiring the Swedish group's solid and successful heavy trucks unit. Ford's current focus is on vehicles which people can drive with a standard driver's license. Period.

Ford's luxury brands – which include Jaguar, Lincoln and Aston Martin as well as Volvo – will be combined into the Premier Automotive Group, based in Europe and headed by former BMW executive Wolfgang Reitzle. To help invigorate the rest of the company as well, Ford CEO Jacques Nasser has hired outsiders for key positions and has made top officials' compensation dependent on stock performance.

The company's share price rose by almost 90 percent in 1998, but hovered at around $60 per share in early 1999 despite record profits and unit sales.

Ford can be found at **www2.ford.com**

The vision which guides Ford, however, will not necessarily transfer to another automobile maker. DaimlerChrysler, for instance, makes heavy trucks and owns the Freightliner unit which purchased Ford's heavy trucks business. One might be tempted, then, to ask who has the better vision, Ford or DaimlerChrysler? This question, however, misses the point about the process of creating a vision.

> **The new rule:** guide post-merger integration with a clear and realistic vision derived from thorough business due diligence.

Visions are not peel-off labels which can be transferred from one company to another. Developing a proper vision is an organic process based on a comprehensive business due diligence which addresses customers, capabilities, competitors, costs and culture. The results of these analyses can and often should vary significantly from company to company. They will lead, then, to different visions, each inherently viable in its own right.

The credibility of a properly developed "one business" vision is crucial to achieving the necessary buy-in, to give the newly-merged organization a clear and understandable orientation tailored to its situation, and to create positive yet realistic expectations within the new organization.

What you have to do

- **Define what you can do.** This involves assessing not only what you possess in terms of competitive advantages, research capabilities and other resources, but what your merger partner can do as well. This knowledge comes from a thorough business due diligence which is market-oriented, not just financial-oriented.

- **Define where you want to go.** What markets do you want to be active in? Where can you best bring the combined abilities of your new organization to bear, and in the process create something new and powerful?

- **Remain realistic.** Credibility and clarity are crucial to the creation of a bold vision. A statement which is unclear or unrealistic will not generate buy-in and will not be followed.

- **Don't copy or co-opt.** The best visions cannot be transferred like labels from one company to another. There must be something with which the company's employees and customers can uniquely identify, based on the credibility and clarity of the statement.

- **Communicate constantly.** Visions live. Whether you call them a touchstone or an acid test, they serve as a control and a check on the major – and in some cases minor – moves your new organization will take. Proper and continual communication throughout the organization will prompt your employees to ask themselves "Is that us?" or "Is that what we really want to do?" when they take a decision.

- **Let "fit" follow.** If you have followed the guidelines above, it seems only natural that the issues of fit in all their various forms – from financial to strategic – should follow from the overall vision. Trying it the other way around does not work.

RULE 2

Leadership

It's critical. Establish it quickly!

Summary

Leadership is the most urgent priority when a merger closes. The faster a merged company can establish its management – by working out compromises, minimizing or preventing defections, and making the most of available talent and knowledge – the faster the company can take advantage of the growth opportunities inherent in its "one business" vision.

Our study revealed the following fact.

✳ **Fact: speed matters.**
Leadership's urgency is often neglected. Some 39 percent of all companies faced a leadership vacuum because they failed to make the establishment of leadership a priority. They experienced major problems as a result, because they failed to obtain buy-in and they had no way to provide a clear orientation. Conflicts simmer, decisions fail to be taken, and constituencies – from employees to customers to market analysts – lose patience.

The new rule regarding leadership in post-merger integration is: do it fast to avoid a leadership vacuum and to move the integration process forward! Forget the old timetables and the old milestones.

You and your merger partner have reached a tentative agreement on the details of the friendly pooling of interests which will create your new entity. You have just delegated the detail work to the lawyers and investment bankers, which frees you and your counterparts to address some of the non-financial questions, like getting in front of the troops.

In your briefcase are packets of slides, which flesh out some of the benefits of the merger. You and your team have already invested considerable time in defining the many cost-saving and growth opportunities your new company could have.

You did not, however, give any thought to the political minefield your merger created. And the mines are everywhere.

First, the CEO of your merger partner, now your chief operating officer (COO), has prepared a similar set of slides. The title page is the same and presents the agreed vision of the new company in unmistakable bold letters. But after the title page, there is no similarity at all. Her slides show different suggestions for milestones, a different hierarchy, a set of goals which conflict with yours, and some strong suggestions on how to handle the "soft" issues like culture.

Oh, and by the way, the schedule has been altered. She – not you – will present first, because she has another appointment across town, where she plans to be the key speaker at a town-hall meeting addressing employees at "your" main R&D facility. You got the voice-mail message, didn't you? Her VP of Operations and her chief financial officer (CFO) will sit in and take notes at your presentation, she says, adding something about "empowerment" and "that's the way I do things."

Twenty minutes ago you thought the division of power in the new company was settled. Wasn't it you who – to begin with – planned to see all major operations globally within the first 45 days of the merger? Wasn't it you who was going to explain the merger rationale to the employees in person and answer all their questions? You feel yourself staring into a vacuum, and right now your counterpart and her team are moving rapidly to fill it.

Post-merger integration demands leadership. The greatest "one business" vision imaginable is worthless if you fail to apply it and execute it properly. The first steps toward execution begin with leadership, first with the appointment of the top management team and then – successively and quickly – the levels immediately below. These newly-appointed key executives must then "walk the talk" and become leaders of the integration. This allows for transparency, which will in turn create acceptance. You must avoid – even for a moment – allowing a vacuum in leadership to develop.

Anyone who has experienced a successful post-merger integration process will remember what can be understood as the common denominator of such a process: speed. Putting the management team in place quickly brings benefits that are otherwise extremely difficult to capture. The common wisdom regarding the establishment of a high-level management team says you need to move quickly, but it captures neither the urgency of this step, nor explains the consequences when it is not followed.

> A merger without strong leadership in place from its early days – and preferably *before* its early days – will drift quickly. And drift is deadly.

But then again, how often is this common wisdom even used? A merger without strong leadership in place from its early days – and preferably *before* its early days – will drift quickly. And drift is deadly.

Charisma and decisiveness help prevent a vacuum from emerging

The top leadership level of the newly-merged organization should be in place within one week after the consummation of the deal. The management layer immediately below top management should be named and approved within 30 days after that consummation. Finally, middle management should be up and running within the first 90 days of the merger integration process.

That all sounds like simple advice, but following it demands firm decisions. That probably explains the fact revealed by our survey.

✳ **Fact:** speed matters.

This means that leadership's urgency is often neglected. Some 39 percent of all companies fail to establish leadership fast, and experience major problems as a result.

What goes wrong here? In some cases the companies completely fail to make the tough decisions to build a management team in a timely manner. This leads to uncertainty in the workforce, rumors, and consequently panic-stricken reactions. Well-qualified people tend to leave in such a situation. Or customers start to re-orient. They begin to think that they may feel better off with another supplier. In other cases, an acceptable plan is developed with the right staffing and timing aspects, but the team does not gel and the members do not work together. This is often the case in a "merger of equals" situation.

Many of the remaining 61 percent who made the effort to follow guidelines simply did not move as fast as they should or could have. They may eventually name a leadership team, with great people, just the right experienced personalities with an eagerness to change things. But the train has already left the station. The leaders cannot integrate a workforce that is already in dissolution.

The global pharmaceutical industry has experienced rapid consolidation in the last several years. Four particular mega-mergers that have been announced since 1995 illustrate the importance of establishing leadership immediately. Two of these mergers were scrapped before consummation precisely because the two companies were unable to agree on who would lead the merged company.

In 1998, the case of *Monsanto-American Home Products* and that of *Glaxo Wellcome-SmithKline Beecham* should serve as a warning to those who fail to take leadership aspects seriously. The Glaxo case is discussed in the "culture" section, but we introduce Monsanto here.

Monsanto and American Home Products

In June 1998 Monsanto and American Home Products (AHP) unveiled a $35-billion merger which on the surface had plenty to offer both companies. The deal would have combined Monsanto's pipeline of drugs and biotechnology products with the sales and marketing strength of AHP.

The merger fell through in October 1998. Neither side made a disclosure of the reasons, beyond saying that the deal was no longer in the best interests of shareholders. Speculation, however, pointed to an impending power struggle between Monsanto CEO Robert Shapiro and his counterpart at AHP, John Stafford. What made the companies complement each other so well on the product and sales side gave them the potential to clash on the cultural side. Monsanto is known more for its recent risk-taking, whereas AHP has a more conservative, cost-oriented reputation.

Monsanto can be found at **www.monsanto.com**
American Home Products can be found at **www.ahp.com**

Leadership has to be established. It has to be demonstrated, and it has to be shared. Decisions are not made in a vacuum. Nor do they just "happen." This holds true in particular for decisions which need to be made fast and firmly to preserve the momentum of a fresh merger and to help it make its first moves toward long-term success.

> It is virtually impossible for a CEO or president of a company to successfully delegate the responsibility of installing a management team.

It is virtually impossible for a CEO or president of a company to successfully delegate the responsibility of installing a management team and ensuring it has the mandate, the confidence from above, and the necessary buy-in to get things done. Delegation would be tantamount to abdication of a serious responsibility.

We are not going to call attention to the "strong man" theory here, and claim that the only time a merger has a chance of success is when the acquiring company is run by a charismatic, respected, top-drawer, and powerful CEO. Though there are several examples of mergers which are seemingly successful precisely because a Michael Eisner or Percy Barnevik was in charge, the point is not to have the business equivalent of a household name at the helm. In many cases, this "charismatic" leadership is not a given. The point is that someone needs to step up, face the decisions, and take them. This might mean accepting a decrease in popularity. It could also mean accepting, for a short while, that old followers may turn against the new leader as he or she does what is needed for the new company.

A pharmaceutical merger which drifted for years until someone took the reins is Pharmacia & Upjohn, which united Sweden's Pharmacia AB with US-based Upjohn in 1995. The situation immediately following this merger of equals was typical in many respects.

Pharmacia and Upjohn

After Sweden's Pharmacia AB and US-based Upjohn Co merged in November 1995, considerable discrepancies emerged among the Swedish and American managers. The decision to move the headquarters of the new company to "neutral" London was meant to show that neither company would have a clear upper hand in what was described as a "merger of equals." But the conflicts arose following the decision to make Upjohn's CEO, John Zabriskie, CEO of Pharmacia & Upjohn and Jan Ekberg, CEO of Pharmacia, the non-executive chairman.

The discontent among the Swedish managers – who were used to a more co-operative management style – prompted more and more of them to leave the company. Zabriskie himself departed in January 1997. In a little over one year, the company's share price had fallen by almost 40 percent to around $28.

The restructuring plan initiated by new CEO Fred Hassan in 1997 called for cost savings, R&D investment, and a larger sales force. The company's share price more than doubled between the second quarter of 1997 and the second quarter of 1999, as Pharmacia & Upjohn began to show consistent earnings growth.

Pharmacia & Upjohn can be found at **www.pnu.com**

Pharmacia & Upjohn is only now making strides toward capturing the long-sought synergies the merger promised. This can be attributed to the efforts of Fred Hassan, who has run the company since 1997. Hassan, who joined the company from American Home Products, began his tenure by doing exactly what should have been done two years earlier.

- He instantly took control.

- He had a strategic plan developed within nine weeks.

- His first step was naming a new senior management team.

To facilitate decision making, Hassan's management team was smaller. It combined members of the former team with talent recruited from outside. The healing effects – both within management and within the company – were almost immediate.

A favorable start is no reason for complacency

Not all mergers drift like Pharmacia & Upjohn did. Decisions in an unsupportive, uncertain environment are never easy. But even when the climate is relatively co-operative and friendly, there is absolutely no room for complacent leaders. Companies cannot afford to take their time, or place less emphasis on establishing their top management quickly, just because the deal begins with a positive impetus.

Novartis, the company formed when Swiss pharmaceutical giants

Ciba-Geigy and Sandoz merged, represents an example of a company which successfully put its management team in place right at the outset. This enabled them to reap other benefits quickly. The relationship between the two partners was less tense than in other merger environments, but the people in charge nonetheless reacted with the required firmness and quickness. The deal had been highly confidential up until its announcement, but an exceptionally high number of integration issues were resolved during this secret, pre-merger phase.

Novartis

During the three months from the start of the negotiations until the announcement of the deal in 1996, the merger partners Ciba-Geigy and Sandoz demonstrated effective leadership through a number of decisions. These decisions included the staffing of key positions, the determination of the business units to be divested, and the new company name. Their action helped to minimize the period of uncertainty for all constituencies.

The merger's main objective was to focus more strongly on the health, agriculture and nutrition areas. Further goals included cost savings of $1.7 billion and the strengthening of R&D by combining the capacities of both predecessor companies. The new management style approximated Ciba's lean hierarchies.

Net profits and cash flow rose strongly in the first joint business year. Sales showed a slight increase, and the company slightly exceeded its cost savings target for 1997. Sales then rose by an additional 2 percent in 1998 to around $24 billion, while net profit climbed by 16 percent to roughly $4 billion. By the end of 1998, the company claimed it had completed 89 percent of its overall cost savings program.

Before falling back in early 1999, the company's share price had risen by almost 90 percent since the fourth quarter 1996.

Novartis can be found at **www.novartis.com**

The leaders at Novartis paid special attention to defining management roles quickly and communicating them confidently and clearly.

One example of the ability to take decisions in an adverse climate and make a post-merger integration process successful through the establishment of leadership is the 1997 merger of another pair of Swiss companies, this time in the banking sector. Union Bank of Switzerland (UBS) and Swiss Bank Corporation (SBC) merged to form United Bank of Switzerland, the world's second largest bank in terms of total assets. Cost savings of between $2 billion and $2.5 billion from scale and capital benefits were anticipated, as well as growth in the investment and international banking sectors. But the focus soon shifted to management.

United Bank of Switzerland

Swiss Bank Corporation (SBC) would hold only 40 percent of the shares in the new United Bank of Switzerland, but it took on a very dominant role in the staffing of the executive positions. Marcel Ospel, the former CEO of SBC, also became CEO of the new company. In addition to this key position, SBC provided majorities on several important boards and committees.

This "takeover" in 1997 by SBC initially caused uncertainty and discontent among the staff at the partner, Union Bank of Switzerland. In spite of this potentially negative climate, Ospel avoided an exodus of executives by publishing the organizational charts and the names of the selected executives on the first two management levels at the very first press conference. Three months later, some 2,000 key positions were filled, thus securing the company's top people.

The company's performance reached only the low end of expectations for 1998, with a profit of around $2 billion. In announcing the company's first quarter 1999 results, however, Ospel claimed that the merger was "largely digested." Net profit at the bank rose by 21 percent to 1.62 billion Swiss francs.

Results for 1999 are expected to continue to improve thanks to a renewed focus on core competencies, as demonstrated by the divestment of assets such as a 75 percent stake in precious metals processor Argor-Heraeus SA and the decision to sell off selected real estate holdings.

The company's stock price fell to $197 per share from $477 in 1998, but has since climbed steadily and reached $385 early in the second quarter of 1999.

United Bank of Switzerland can be found at **www.ubs.com**

Sometimes someone needs to take a back seat

Standing up and taking control is necessary in the post-merger phase to keep a leadership vacuum from emerging. But in some cases – especially in the so-called "merger of equals" – the competition to fill that vacuum can be intense and even destructive.

Companies take different steps to solve this problem. In the case of Monsanto and American Home Products, they called the merger off. In cases such as DaimlerChrysler and Citigroup, they operated through the integration phase with two CEOs. Companies can go outside their combined ranks to bring in a third party, or they can reach an agreement where one merger partner's CEO takes a subordinate role to the other. This latter approach is thought to have rescued the now successful merger between the US investment bank Morgan Stanley and the brokerage house Dean Witter.

Morgan Stanley Dean Witter

The companies' core businesses (underwriting and retail financial services) differed, but Morgan Stanley and Dean Witter nonetheless decided to call their February 1997 union a "merger of equals."

Morgan Stanley ranks alongside Goldman Sachs and Merrill Lynch as one of the top, traditional Wall Street investment banks, while Dean Witter – spun off from retailer Sears, Roebuck in 1993 – had a broad customer base in retail brokerage as well as the Discover credit card business. In this sense, one could view the merger as forward integration on the part of Morgan Stanley.

The potentially volatile question of who would run the company was diffused when Morgan Stanley CEO John Mack decided not to challenge Dean Witter CEO Phil Purcell for the top job. A co-CEO arrangement or a fight for the top job may have hindered the integration process or killed the merger entirely.

The integration process continues, but the company did demonstrate its cross-selling capabilities when Morgan Stanley underwrote an initial public offering (IPO) for the oil company Conoco, formerly a unit of US chemical giant DuPont. The Dean Witter network of retail brokers took over 10 percent of the issue, which was valued at over $4 billion and was the largest IPO in US history.

Since October 1998, the common stock of Morgan Stanley Dean Witter has risen from $37 per share to over $100.

Morgan Stanley Dean Witter can be found at **www.msdw.com**

The decision to "hold back" puts the needs of the merger at the forefront. But even when there is virtually no competition for the top job, a certain sense of "holding back" is sometimes called for to ensure that the employees of the merger partner do not feel overwhelmed. Claude Bebear, the CEO of the French insurance group Axa, sensed the need for a clear yet softer form of leadership when his company took over the struggling US insurer Equitable in 1991.

Axa and Equitable

Equitable Companies, one of the oldest names in life insurance in the United States, was struggling in the late 1980s amidst a looming recession and downturns in the markets for real estate and high-yield bonds. At the same time, Axa, a French life insurer with a history stretching back over 150 years, was looking for opportunities to enter the US market.

Axa CEO Claude Bebear and Equitable Chairman Richard Jenrette signed a merger agreement in 1991, under which Axa would invest over $1 billion for a 60 percent stake in Equitable. The resulting integration of the two companies was described by a former Axa vice-president as "as smooth as any merger of cultures I'm aware of." This success can be attributed in part to Bebear's leadership, under which Equitable was viewed more as a partner than an acquisition target.

Sensitive to the potential for culture clash in a cross-border merger, Bebear led according to the motto of "Everything but ..." In other words, he left considerable independence and autonomy with Equitable employees and agents.

Axa now operates in 50 countries. It ranks as Europe's second-largest insurance group behind Germany's Allianz AG, and derives 32 percent of its annual revenues from North America.

Axa can be found at **www.axa.com**

Sometimes, however, the match is not so easy to make. Either the CEOs cannot agree on who will take charge, or feel that there will be unavoidable "us versus them" backlashes if one CEO "wins" and the other receives another high-level position but actually "loses." In this case, it sometimes makes sense to go entirely outside the organization to bring in a leader who is capable of pushing the merger forward by taking the steps which increase buy-in and place the focus on growth. Another alternative is to use a double CEO.

> It sometimes makes sense to go entirely outside the organization to bring in a leader who is capable of pushing the merger forward.

The intensely watched merger which combined Germany's Daimler-Benz and the third-largest US automaker Chrysler Corporation is in many ways a model of post-merger integration thus far. Like the merger which formed Novartis, this deal was planned carefully and confidentially over many months.

But in contrast to Novartis, DaimlerChrysler presented unprecedented challenges, due in part to its status as the largest transatlantic merger in history, valued at an estimated $40 billion. Nonetheless, Chairmen Juergen Schrempp and Robert Eaton had many positive results to announce just two months after the merger closed in November 1998.

DaimlerChrysler

Juergen Schrempp and Robert Eaton understand the new rule on establishing leadership, and they have followed it to the letter. They turned the naming of top management and the development of a new organizational structure into a top priority of post-merger integration. And they accomplished it with unexpected swiftness.

Schrempp and Eaton jointly demonstrated leadership and took care of the "who," "what," and "how" questions flying around. In the first 55 days after the merger, DaimlerChrysler filled all its top management posts, defined its worldwide marketing and sales structure, and finalized the company's brand policy. It also set its procurement strategy and began a company-wide development program for top managers.

These tasks had been complicated by the level of compensation received by former Chrysler managers, who had earned considerably more than their German counterparts. A new compensation structure was worked out for 250 top managers in Germany in order to offer them incentives and opportunities in line with American custom.

The company reported a 12 percent gain in sales and a 19 percent gain in net profit for 1998, while expanding its staff by 4 percent to around 441,000. While the company's share price has come down from all-time highs, it still stood over 10 percent above its initial launch price by July 1999.

DaimlerChrysler can be found at **www.daimlerchrysler.com**

The decision on who will run the company is the largest make-or-break decision in the early stages of the merger. This decision will always be dependent on the sensitivities involved, as well as the due diligence input. In any event, the ultimate outcome must be a quick decision which establishes clear lines of authority and eliminates the chance that a vacuum could arise.

> The decision on who will run the company is the largest make-or-break decision in the early stages of the merger.

Background checks as part of the leadership selection process may be controversial, but nonetheless form an essential part of the due diligence when the upper management ranks are filled. Prior to the completion of their merger, the US oil giants Exxon and Mobil had already begun their human resources due diligence. When the hurdles of shareholder and regulatory approval are finally crossed, Exxon Mobil should be well-positioned to "keep the keepers."

Exxon Mobil

The merger between these two former units of Standard Oil would create a global petroleum and chemical company with a market capitalization of $265 billion, making it one of the largest mergers in US history. Staff consolidation among the combined company's 120,000 employees is inevitable. The partners, however, are taking advantage of the time between the merger announcement in November 1998 and the anticipated regulatory approval in 1999 to deepen their due diligence efforts to help determine which personnel should be retained.

The analysts' view is that the company's ability to maintain key personnel – in other words, to "keep the keepers" – is especially important at Mobil, which is the target company in the merger and is roughly half of Exxon's size. The current due diligence effort involves over 20 transition teams who are gathering and processing background information on key employees. Mobil, meanwhile, has been preparing incentive plans to ensure that staff remain in place at least until the merger is completed and the full integration process can begin.

Exxon can be found at **www.exxon.com**
Mobil can be found at **www.mobil.com**

No matter whom you choose, move quickly

Speed matters. The benefits of responding fast and decisively are numerous. First of all, you do not leave your stakeholders hanging, and you leave no room for speculation or rumor. The stock market receives clear signals on how the company will be managed, and the employees know who is in charge. This positive signal helps generate buy-in for the merger, and shows where the orientation for stakeholders will come from. Otherwise, anxiety and uncertainty will grow significantly over time. Decisions postponed – especially when management lines are unclear – will come back to haunt you.

Two companies that announced mergers in 1998 have understood the urgency of establishing leadership quickly. One had its team announced before the merger was even closed, while the other wasted no time after the completion of the deal in making it clear who reports to whom.

Universal Music Group

Few industries have undergone a longer and more active consolidation process than a special "software" or "content" industry: recorded music. The $40 billion global market for recorded music is already dominated by just a few firms who have collected many entrepreneurial and successful labels – from Motown to Geffen to Island – and combined them into massive entertainment groups.

This trend moved even further forward in 1998, when the Canada-based drinks-and-entertainment group Seagram's Ltd purchased Polygram Records from the Dutch electronics group Philips NV for around $10.6 billion.

Polygram would be merged into Seagram's Universal unit to form a behemoth which would own over 650,000 individual copyrights and would hold an estimated 23 percent of the global music market. It would rank as the world's third largest publishing entity.

In an industry where people mean everything, the new Universal Music Group (UMG) took virtually no time at all to establish its management teams and its reporting lines. Within two weeks after Seagram's tender offer for the outstanding shares of Polygram closed, UMG announced the location of six regional headquarters and the labels for which they would be responsible. It also introduced the nine people who would head various divisions, drawn from both Universal and Polygram staff.

The stock of the parent company, Seagram, has almost doubled since October 1998. In spring 1999, the company announced the creation of an on-line music store in co-operation with Germany's Bertelsmann. The move is meant to challenge on-line music retailers such as amazon.com.

Universal Music Group can be found at **www.universalstudios.com/music**

The new rule for leadership is to handle it as the central issue before closing the deal – no "vacuums" at any time.

Another company, US-based International Paper, leverages its experience from previous acquisition projects. Its latest merger involved the integrated paper producer Union Camp. The merger had not yet closed when the two companies announced that the leadership structure for the combined firm had been established.

International Paper and Union Camp

In November 1998, International Paper (IP) Chairman and CEO John Dillon told Wall Street analysts that the company would seek to grow by making targeted acquisitions. The 100-year-old company, which sells its products in over 130 countries worldwide and is a component of the Dow Jones average of 30 industrials, sought to sharpen its focus on customers while keeping an eye on product quality and innovation.

Just two weeks after Dillon's comments, the company unveiled the $7.9 billion friendly acquisition of rival Union Camp. The deal came two years after IP successfully integrated Federal Paper, another smaller rival.

What stood out in the handling of the merger was that the management team – not just at the top level, but also in the geographical and product units – was announced 45 days before the merger even became official.

The deal was finally approved by shareholders of both companies in April 1999. International Paper's share price rose by over 35 percent in the first four months of 1999, while Union Camp's more than doubled from $34 in September 1998 to $79 at the end of April 1999.

International Paper can be found at **www.internationalpaper.com**

The best "one-business" vision in the world is useless unless the right management team can begin applying it as quickly as possible.

What you have to do

If you are undecided about what to do with respect to leadership, make sure you do at least three things.

- **Decisively put a leadership blueprint in place prior to closing.** Leadership patterns have to be communicated, understood, and accepted.

- **"Keep the keepers."** The top managerial talent in the combined organization should already have been identified in your business due diligence. Whether you can simply convince them to stay or whether you need "golden handcuffs," you need to lock in the top talent immediately.

- **Act as quickly as your situation dictates.** The key word here is "speed." Throw out the old timetable. This calls for a specific feel for timing.

RULE 3

Growth

You merge in order to grow –
focus on the added value

Summary

The new rule regarding cost-cutting and similar synergies in mergers and acquisitions is to make them a secondary issue in the post-merger integration. We cannot deny that almost all mergers offer opportunities to save money. But the primary reason for the merger decision – and the obvious focal point during post-merger integration – should be growth.

Growth means unlocking the "merger added value" by taking advantage of the positive combinations offered by the company's combined resources, ie taking advantage of "growth" synergies identified in your due diligence. By placing too much emphasis on "cost" or "efficiency" synergies, companies drown out their growth story and run the risk of cutting too much and for too long.

In short, there are two kinds of synergies: "efficiency" and "growth." Our survey clearly shows where the emphasis currently – and unfortunately – lies.

✳ **Fact one: cost-cutting is too often the focus.**
Some 76 percent of companies surveyed focused too heavily on the "efficiency" synergies.

✳ **Fact two: growth opportunities get ignored.**
Some 30 percent of the companies surveyed virtually ignored attractive growth opportunities such as cross-selling possibilities or knowledge sharing in research and development.

Four months ago you gave a select team a clear mandate: explore a small set of strategic opportunities and find us a merger partner or acquisition candidate. Today they have just shown you the best strategic opportunity, and have described the three merger partners they are recommending.

The back-up data for each recommended company includes a thumb-thick stack of charts breaking down the millions of dollars in synergies which each merger would offer. The numbers look attractive, and you have already stopped counting the number of times your controller has either smiled, nodded, or eagerly taken notes in the last 30 minutes.

The team leader has now invited discussion. After a brief pause, the first hand goes up.

"With all these charts about synergies, what you are really talking about at the end of the day is cost-cutting, right?"

"Exactly," the team leader responds, quickly placing a summary slide on the overhead projector. As he once again goes through the details – $10 million here, $55 million there, etc, etc – you begin formulating your own question. When the explanation ends, you jump in with a question that immediately drains the excitement from the room.

"And then what?" you ask calmly. "What happens next? What happens after we've cut?"

Despite his considerable experience and his rhetorical skills, the team leader has a hard time disguising the fact that he is struggling to come up with an answer. Meanwhile, your controller looks quizzically at you, then to the team leader, then back to you again. Finally, the answer comes.

"To be perfectly honest: I don't quite get the question."

Ever since the last merger wave in the late 1980s, hardly a press release gets written by one of the merging companies without some hard reference to the money to be saved because of "synergies." The word "growth" almost never receives top billing ahead of synergies, if growth is even mentioned at all.

Synergy, as you might have already guessed, ranks alongside "fit" as one of the most mythical, confusing, deluding words in the business world. For if "fit" is the imp whispering in the CEO's or the investment banker's ear, "synergy" is usually the snake oil the imp is trying to peddle. Synergy is often treated as a synonym for cost-cutting and a euphemism for job cuts and factory shutdowns.

This is unfortunate, because almost all well-researched and well-planned mergers will come loaded with two types of synergy potential: "efficiency," which involves cost savings and which draws all the attention, and "growth," the market-oriented synergies where the upside lies.

Despite such a positive starting situation, merged companies are rarely successful in capitalizing on the synergies they proclaimed prior to striking the deal. The companies either go about their efforts wrongly, or focus solely on achieving anticipated efficiency synergies at the expense of the growth synergies. Common misconceptions cloud managers' thinking. Among them is the belief that the merged company will have to undergo a slump in sales and shrink before consolidating and starting to grow.

We will elaborate on ways you can look for, recognize, and take advantage of the growth synergies that really matter and that should have helped drive your merger decision to begin with. The time and resources spent on achieving efficiency synergies should be kept to the minimum necessary, so that the upside opportunities offered by the "growth" synergies are not overlooked or missed.

We have found in our research that mergers – despite their high failure rate and the negative statistics we cite in this book – offer an excellent way for companies to realize their growth plans. Comparing growth by acquisition to the more traditional and often favored "organic" growth, we find refreshing news. Growth by acquisition can be just as effective as an in-house-driven effort to grow your company. In some cases it may even save the time that the organic growers use for "spiraling up," which means growing and then falling back a bit before growing again.

> Growth by acquisition can be just as effective as an in-house-driven effort to grow your company.

This offers a very positive perspective to all who have an acquisition or merger in mind. But our caveat remains: post-merger integration is the key to professionally unlocking your growth opportunities. It must be done properly, thoroughly, and decisively.

Synergy suicide: cost reduction is not a driving force

Efficiency synergies are still very much at the center of merger philosophies. But the reality of post-merger integration calls efficiency synergies into doubt as the focus or driving force behind a merger. First of all, such synergies have rarely been realized in full in most mergers anyway. And even when they are achieved, there is absolutely no correlation between successful cost-cutting after a merger and the merger's ultimate chances of survival.

Ironically, one company did indeed meet nearly every efficiency synergy it proposed, but its pursuit hit some obstacles which hampered the merger's success. The 1996 merger between US banks Wells Fargo & Co and First Interstate Bancorp shows that curing the disease can almost kill the patient.

Wells Fargo & Co / First Interstate Bancorp

When these two competitors merged in an $11.3 billion transaction in 1996, the considerable overlap of the California-based banks' branch networks led to expectations of $800 million in efficiency synergies from savings in operating costs. These were achieved in part by cutting 20 percent of the workforce by the end of 1996.

Wells Fargo also discovered considerable savings potential in information technology. Wanting to move quickly, it set a deadline of only seven months for integrating the computer system of all First Interstate Bancorp branches. It nearly reached the goal, but the effort harmed internal and customer relationships. The company later attributed a decline in operating profit to back-office problems resulting from the First Interstate integration.

If the share price is any indication, the First Interstate merger ultimately proved to be successful. Wells Fargo shares have almost doubled since 1996. At the end of

1998, the company announced a merger with Norwest, a successful regional bank. To smooth integration and reduce uncertainty, the company has launched several merger-related pages on its home page.

Wells Fargo can be found at **www.wellsfargo.com**

In business reality, it is very hard to strike the balance between the work of making the newly-merged company more efficient – which flows through to the bottom line – and making the company grow, which influences both the top and bottom lines. Nowadays the balance tends to be stacked in favor of efficiency.

* **Fact one:** cost-cutting is too often the focus.

Our Global PMI survey showed that 76 percent of companies place their emphasis on efficiency synergies. Nonetheless, most fail to make full use of existing synergies or make unsuccessful or half-hearted attempts to realize them.

Instead of concentrating on the growth synergies, top management of these companies is primarily interested in the efficiency gains offered by savings potential. At some inflection point, however, all of this cost-cutting and job slashing triggers substantial shrinkage instead of substantial growth. The Wells Fargo case of cost savings – whether accidental or not – is an illustrative warning.

Even though lean is still beautiful, companies that overemphasize this objective will shrink to death, taking a small but significant part of their national economy with them.

* **Fact two:** growth opportunities get ignored.

Some 30 percent of companies surveyed virtually ignored attractive growth opportunities such as cross-selling possibilities or knowledge sharing in research and development.

Growth must take center stage in the merger

A strong example of a growth-oriented merger is the 1996 deal which combined the US consumer products giant Gillette with the leading alkaline battery maker Duracell. Gillette looks for companies to acquire in order to meet its growth targets. While many companies would have "fit" well to Gillette, and would benefit from its marketing and distribution expertise, the growth vision mattered when it acquired Duracell's leading position in alkaline batteries.

Gillette and Duracell

Look for a company with a convincing growth story, and you need look no further than Boston, Massachusetts, where Gillette has been based for around 100 years.

Gillette is recognized worldwide as a company that knows what it wants, what it can do, and where it is headed. The manufacturer and marketer of "value-added personal care and personal use" products strives to be number one or number two in every market in which it competes.

It accomplishes this not only through intensive research and development, but also through marketing and – above all – distribution expertise. Gillette's network makes its razor blades available virtually anywhere on the globe. The company estimates that 1.2 billion people – more than 20 percent of the world's population – use at least one Gillette product every day.

In late 1996, Gillette acquired Duracell for around $7.2 billion in what it described from the outset as an ideal cross-selling opportunity. The company said it could not only build on Duracell's leading position in alkaline batteries in the United States, but it could tap global opportunities as well.

The effect was almost immediate. Duracell's sales – in a market facing a stiff headwind – grew by 10 percent in 1997, thanks largely to Gillette's ability to quickly and effectively place the Duracell products in its network. The first-year results exceeded even Gillette's own high expectations.

Warren Buffett, who sits on Gillette's board, prefers companies that make products or provide services that people will still need years and years from now. People will always need to shave. In the future, it appears they will also have a huge appetite for batteries to power their pagers, mobile phones, portable CD players – and even their flashlights from time to time.

Gillette can be found at **www.gillette.com**
Duracell can still be reached at **www.duracell.com**

All top managers involved in a merger in whatever position must understand that merging does not automatically mean growth. It may even result in shrinkage, if swift actions are not taken to tear down the barriers impeding solid and healthy growth.

> The term "synergies" must be redefined to go beyond cost-cutting "efficiency" and include the pursuit of the positive, growth-oriented aspects of the merger.

The idea that a company needs to have a temporary decline in combined revenues after the merger is a myth. It has no basis. Furthermore, the term "synergies" must be redefined to go beyond cost-cutting "efficiency" and include the pursuit of the positive, growth-oriented aspects of the merger.

Exxon and Mobil have taken precisely this step in the planning of their post-merger integration. The exact timing of their merger may have been precipitated by external factors such as low oil prices and the announcement of the merger between rivals British Petroleum and Amoco. Exxon and Mobil officials, however, view the striking of a proper balance between efficiency and growth synergies as the primary rationale behind their merger and the ultimate determinant of its success.

Exxon Mobil

When these two global oil producers announced their merger in November 1998, observers focused on one number: the proposed $2.8 billion in cost savings which the companies planned to make. Two-thirds of this amount would come from eliminating duplication and excess capacity, realigning operations, and reducing the workforce.

The growth opportunities – which both companies claim to be the true rationale behind the merger – may not have received the attention they deserved. These opportunities arose because the two companies are highly complementary in many areas. By sharing expertise and reorganizing the new, combined company along product and service lines rather than geographic lines, Exxon Mobil can now focus and invest its available resources in an optimal set of projects, both upstream and downstream. As separate companies, for example, one would have held rights to explore certain fields but would have lacked the other company's proprietary technology to make those fields productive even at low oil price levels.

As Exxon and Mobil succinctly put it, their merger brings two types of benefits: near-term operating synergies (ie efficiency synergies) and better returns due to the ability to fund a greater number of long-term growth projects (ie growth synergies). The latter will give the company a stronger and more balanced position in high-growth areas such as natural gas.

The merger still awaits regulatory approval, but the market has already responded positively. Thanks as well to a recent rise in crude oil prices, the aggregate market capitalization of the two companies has risen to $265 billion in July 1999 from $238 billion when the deal was announced less than nine months earlier.

Exxon can be found at **www.exxon.com**
Mobil can be found at **www.mobil.com**

A classical stream merger with growth at the forefront is the deal which brought Disney and American Broadcasting Corp (ABC) together via Disney's purchase of Capital Cities.

ABC's position had eroded since the days when it, NBC, and CBS ruled television in the United States. But the company still controls a wide range of media outlets which Disney can use to distribute its programming. This would provide another growth outlet for Disney, which

– simply because of its breadth and size – had reached certain saturation points in other areas.

Walt Disney Company

Walt Disney took over Capital Cities/ABC Inc in February 1996 for $19 billion with the intention of expanding its entertainment activities into the distribution sector. Through the deal, the company established a link between its theme parks, movie and TV studios, and ABC's radio and TV outlets, through which it would be able to influence broadcasting times and program promotion.

Another goal was the stronger globalization of Disney's activities through the use of ABC's worldwide network. Disney has certain managers whose primary role is to encourage cross-merchandising opportunities in order to maximize the impact of the launches of feature films and television shows. The addition of ABC added yet another major dimension to these opportunities.

There were hardly any overlaps between the two companies and thus only very limited potential for efficiency synergies. The focus for Disney CEO Michael Eisner, however, was on growth anyway. In the reorganization of the combined company following the merger, the new broadcasting unit comprises the Disney Channel as well as ABC units such as the sports network ESPN.

Despite start-up and integration costs, broadcasting's operating profit rose by 3 percent in 1998 to $1.3 billion on revenue growth of 10 percent to $7.1 billion.

Disney can be found at **www.disney.go.com**

Thus far, the move has proved successful for Disney. The merger between Disney and ABC offered the potential for growth, because ABC and its affiliated networks are natural outlets for Disney programming.

Another company which demonstrates the importance of setting clear financial targets, aiming for growth, and ignoring merger myths is the US aluminum company Alcoa. The Pittsburgh-based company has made many domestic and international acquisitions in its effort to reach its ambitious growth targets. The largest of these acquisitions so far was completed in 1998, when the company purchased US rival Alumax for $3.8 billion.

Alcoa

Alcoa wants to become the best aluminum company in the world by pursuing profitable growth. The details reveal a convincing and credible growth story, fueled by acquisition and backed up by strong bottom-line results in a tough, global market.

The Pittsburgh, Pennsylvania-based company took a major step forward when it completed its $3.8 billion purchase of its smaller rival, US-based Alumax, in June 1998. The company closed 1998 with sales of $15 billion and has set a goal of $20 billion by the end of 2000. Alumax already contributed positively to the top and bottom line in its first quarter of integration. In addition to the growth targets, however, Alcoa has set aggressive cost savings targets, including $800 million in operating improvements and $300 million in efficiency synergies from the Alumax purchase.

The optimism permeating these forecasts is reflected in the actual results. While aluminum prices plunged by 20 percent in 1998, Alcoa's sales grew by 15 percent and its net profit by 6 percent. This optimism can be traced back to Paul O'Neill, who is scheduled to retire as Chairman in December 2000. While Warren Buffett might see the world drinking Coca Cola forever, O'Neill seems to feel the world will be drinking all that Coca Cola out of aluminum cans. Where others see overcapacity and falling prices, O'Neill chooses to see opportunities. He notes that current per-capita aluminum use in India and China is just 8 percent of that in the US.

He also considers the increasing use of aluminum in transportation – such as in the frame for the Audi A8 automobile – as the single biggest change in the industry today. Transportation is already Alcoa's largest segment, growing by almost 20 percent in 1998 to $3.7 billion.

The integration process of Alumax is proceeding quickly, and its handling has shown that Alcoa can back up its example of "putting people first" with deeds. It did so by naming a long-time Alumax official to run its existing Australian operations, one of its largest foreign properties.

Alcoa can be found at **www.alcoa.com**

Growth can be achieved even in mature industries

The examples of Gillette, Exxon Mobil, Disney and Alcoa show what can happen when a company merges in order to grow. Backed by convincing and compelling growth stories, these companies demonstrate that a successful merger is driven by the positive growth-oriented synergies, and not the cost-cutting orientation or "efficiency" synergies which have often received the bulk of attention when companies merge.

> **The new rule:** focus on growth – in terms of "merger added value" – and not on efficiency synergies.

Capturing efficiency synergies is important. Duplication needs to be eliminated, and substantial savings can result on many fronts, not just in reduced headcount. But it is ultimately harmful to place too much emphasis on these synergies. The true driver – the make-or-break criterion – is the combined company's ability to prepare itself to grow quickly and strongly while any efficiency synergies are being realized.

Most of the companies mentioned in this section have been around for decades, some for over a century. Batteries, petroleum, and processed aluminum are nothing new and would probably not lead the list of the "sexiest" industries to work in nowadays. Disney, meanwhile, has traditionally held a strong position in entertainment "content," but had begun to reach saturation points after an impressive run-up in revenues and shareholder value which began under Michael Eisner in the mid-1980s.

This is all the more reason for such companies to develop, trumpet and then live up to the believable growth stories which underpin their mergers. Growth, like vision, is not limited to high-tech leaders like Cisco, which is setting new benchmarks in this area.

Cisco Systems

The Fortune 500 list of the largest US companies offers a clear indication of just how rapidly Cisco Systems has grown since its founding in 1984. In the current list the company was ranked 192nd, directly behind traditional computer industry power Texas Instruments.

Thanks to a combination of organic growth and the successful integration of 25 acquisitions, Cisco has almost quadrupled its revenues since 1995 to $8.5 billion and tripled its net income to $1.3 billion. It holds a market share of around 80 percent in the routers and switches which form the Internet infrastructure.

Making acquisitions is and will continue to be absolutely essential for Cisco to maintain its rapid growth and enhance its competitive advantages. As rapidly as technology changes and improves, Cisco could not possibly keep pace over the long term by developing each new product improvement or innovation entirely on its own. Efficiency synergies – to the extent they exist – play a very subordinate role in Cisco's acquisition decisions. The nature of industry means its emphasis must be on growth.

The company's share price rose by 200 percent between October 1998 and July 1999, giving Cisco a market capitalization of $200 billion.

Cisco can be found at **www.cisco.com**

What you have to do

There can be no truly successful merger without growth. The perspective of something positive and expansive creates a much more favorable and optimistic climate than the fear of shrinkage and loss in the aftermath of combining two businesses.

- **Begin capturing growth synergies as early and as quickly as possible.** Growth opportunities should follow directly from the long-term, growth-oriented, "one-business" vision. There are usually growth synergies, ie potential to increase sales quickly in customer, product, and/or geographic segments. These complement the savings potential in shared processes and procurement.

- **Prioritize areas of cost savings.** Your due diligence work, combined with benchmarking, should reveal where the efficiency synergies are located. Find them, prioritize them, and begin realizing them.

RULE 4

Early wins

Act, get results, and communicate –
make tangible, positive moves

Summary

Uncertainty spreads quickly after a merger is announced. It afflicts not only your employees, but suppliers, customers and shareholders as well. Announcements of plans and goals are welcomed, but they are often too long-term to stem the growth of uncertainty.

"Early wins" represent substantial and sustainable moves made quickly after the merger to back up your words with action. They show that improvement is coming. They help you to solidify and expand your buy-in, both inside and outside your new company.

Companies can find early wins internally by looking at areas such as asset sales, knowledge sharing and improvements to the work environment. They can also find a rich source of early wins by looking externally, ie by examining customer and supplier relationships.

✳ **Fact one: most companies look only internally for early wins.**
Very few companies attempt to achieve early wins in an external or outward-looking area, such as in their relationships with suppliers or customers.

✳ **Fact two: companies who look internally often mistake job cuts for early wins.**
Some 61 percent of merged companies search for early wins in the wrong place by focusing on job shedding, factory closings, or other inward-looking cost moves. The emotion attached to such moves can make them backfire and quickly turn them into "early losses."

If your business due diligence has been executed properly and in a timely manner, you should have several levers to pull in order to generate early wins.

Forget your stock options for a moment. You've suddenly got much bigger problems.

Your trade unions are barking about job cuts, which would allegedly violate their collective bargaining agreements. The analysts at the major investment houses are considering whether to change their recommendation on your company's stock from "buy" to "hold" or even to the market's equivalent of the Scarlet Letter: "sell."

Consensus estimates of your profit and sales in the next quarter are lagging behind those of your competitors. Moody's and S&P have put your outstanding debt on watch for a possible downgrade.

On top of that, the US Department of Justice and the European Commission are breathing down your neck about an alleged position of market power and are hinting – in no uncertain terms – that they might require divestitures in return for anti-trust approval of your merger. Which factory will need to close or which subsidiary will need to be sold?

Meanwhile, your competitors are not only courting your key customers, they are also going after your top personnel – from marketing to design to the inner corridors of your highly-prized R&D unit. They have stepped up their media buying to siphon off consumers. And they have engaged two executive search firms who will help them use a few dollar signs to skim off those members of your staff whose heads are currently filled only with question marks.

Finally, you and your merger partner have catapulted yourselves to the number two position in the world market. But instead of doing what you do best – building whatever it was you were successfully building before the merger came along – you now spend most of your time trying to get along with around 35,000 new employees, none of whom know precisely how they should be doing their jobs.

Yours is certainly not an enviable position.

So what do you do in this situation? Fortunately, your pre-merger team performed its due diligence thoroughly and comprehensively. It looked beyond the financial information and pinpointed a number of areas where you can move quickly. Taking action now will show your stakeholders – above all, your employees – that concrete improvement is coming.

T his scenario occurs frequently. As the number of so-called "mega-mergers" increases, it will probably understate the severity and extent of the true set of circumstances.

If you step back for a moment, however, two things begin to become clear. First, you recognize who the true enemy in this situation is. The troublesome party here is certainly not your employees, no matter how hard they press for information or how probing and sharp their questions are. Among your external stakeholders, there are many candidates for an enemy or troublemaker ready to ruin your grand merger plans, but none of them is the root of the problem.

The analysts and market players wield tremendous power, especially in the period shortly after the merger is consummated. There is an element of truth in the tongue-in-cheek wish of American political consultant James Carville, who once remarked that in his next life he would like to be reincarnated as the financial markets, because nothing important in the world can happen without their blessing. But even they have a responsibility to use this power wisely. Union heads and anti-trust lawyers likewise have a job to do and interests to present and defend.

These potential enemies have one thing in common: *uncertainty*, which is the true enemy you need to fight in this situation. The source of this uncertainty is the expectations held by these constituencies. Some of these expectations may be unrealistically high, and some may not be based on the same set of facts and assumptions that have driven your decision to merge. But in all cases, employees and customers do not know whether their expectations will ever be fulfilled.

At the same time, they are understandably restless. They have a very hard time remaining patient as the big changes and successes you have promised in broad brushstrokes take months or years to unfold.

Fight back with deeds, not just with words

The proper offensive against uncertainty in these circumstances is the pursuit of what we call "early wins." These are nuggets of reassurance which send positive signals to all stakeholders and all observers. They reflect substantial and sustainable results. When properly achieved and positively communicated, they serve to create, maintain and expand a store of goodwill. This in turn helps you obtain buy-in and generate the motivation which keeps the merged company moving forward toward the longer-term goals which some may still have a hard time grasping or visualizing.

This may sound like another simple and obvious "common sense" rule. Who can argue with the recommendation that newly-merged companies should strive to achieve early wins to obtain buy-in from the organization?

> Early wins must be properly achieved and positively communicated.

But we have also discovered – once again – that managers find it easy to pay lip service to a standard rule. Actually following the rule is another story entirely. In the last few years the business world has been confronted with a whole slew of billion-dollar deals where the newly-merged company either did not heed this advice or misunderstood it.

Early wins must be properly achieved and positively communicated. Two facts from our Global PMI survey show how often this is ignored.

✳ **Fact one:** most companies look only internally for early wins.

Very few companies attempt to achieve early wins in an outward-looking area, such as in their relationships with suppliers or customers.

The opportunity to optimize supplier relationships or offer customers additional products and services exists in every merger.

✳ **Fact two:** companies mistake job cuts for early wins.

Some 61 percent of the mergers and acquisitions surveyed searched for early wins in the wrong place by focusing on job shedding, factory closings, or other inward-looking cost moves.

We grant that these moves are usually necessary. But we have observed that they are often overemphasized and overpublicized, in addition to taking far too long. These attempts to influence stakeholders are doomed to backfire, because they carry a negative and demotivating connotation. They are also hard for some employees to interpret as wins.

In the previous section we presented companies who have mapped out and pushed a believable, sustainable growth story. Growth, however, takes time. It does not provide you with the immediate ammunition you need to combat your most pressing enemy, which is the urgent uncertainty that inevitably crops up in the days and weeks following the merger.

In this section, we will focus on four areas regarding this ammunition: where to look for it, what to look for, how to gather it, and how to communicate it.

Levers can be found internally *and* externally

Much of the focus in the mistaken search for early wins is on just a few aspects of the cost side. Merged companies will mention job cuts right from the outset, even if they are not sure where they will come and how many jobs will be affected. The same applies for factory closings or the consolidation of departments such as R&D, legal, or human resources.

Think for a moment about the effect such a vague announcement will have.

You are a line employee in a large, foreign-based factory in the newly-merged company. You turn on the evening news program and learn that the rumor you heard at your lunch break has now been confirmed. The new management will need to cut jobs. But did they say in what area? No. Will only administrative jobs be cut, or will manufacturing be hit as well? Who knows. And how many? And when? No answers.

When this is the extent of the information the rank and file employees receive from management, no one should be surprised when anxiety grows as fast as motivation declines. And this will continue as long as your attention – and everyone else's – is focused on playing up the "bad news." Instead, you should be taking action in the areas shown in Fig. 6.

The message here, then, is to work as hard and as quickly as possible to get the cost savings in place. No matter how the various stakeholder groups may state their case or jockey for position, it is usually clear to both sides where the obvious duplication in a merged organization is. This duplication should be removed as quickly as possible, with no indecision and no mixed messages. Its elimination can even be presented as an opportunity for the new organization, which can be "freed up" from excess capacity and redundant positions.

There are two main benefits to completing the necessary cost savings as quickly as possible. First, it shifts your focus from planning to executing. The bulk of what the merger has entailed up to this point has been planning, planning, planning. It is time to act. Second, the comple-

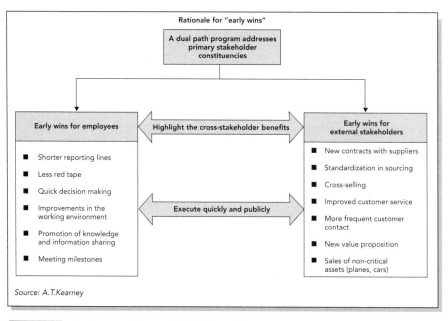

Fig. 6 Early wins for stakeholders follow a dual path (internal and external)

tion of the cost-cutting work paves the way for you to attack the longer-term objectives of the merger, namely the growth-oriented aspects.

The boxes shown in Fig. 6 offer more than enough areas for the early wins you need to combat uncertainty and start earning buy-in. Consider the following example of an improvement in a working environment which led to an immediate leap in employee motivation and ultimately to a dramatically improved performance on the shop floor.

The example below of the transportation services company Penske Corporation and the engine maker Detroit Diesel shows just how quickly you can identify a "win" and just how "early" you can achieve it. Roger Penske, who made his name in automobile racing, took an 80 percent stake in Detroit Diesel, the heavy diesel engine division of General Motors, in 1988. The company was eventually taken public and is now listed on the New York Stock Exchange, but Penske's closely-held Penske Corporation remains the major shareholder.

Detroit Diesel

When automobile racing magnate Roger Penske bought into the ailing Detroit Diesel in 1988, one of his first moves was to visit the manufacturing facilities and get to the root of the company's low productivity and lack of employee motivation.

One thing which stood out in his plant tour was the cafeteria where the line workers took their breaks. The room had all the appeal of a little-used, rural bus station. Plans had previously been drawn up to replace the cafeteria, but they faced weeks or perhaps months of red tape at Detroit Diesel's former parent, General Motors.

Penske immediately decided that the old cafeteria had to go. Very quick research revealed that the company which designs dining areas for McDonald's could also plan and install corporate kitchens and dining facilities. Contact was made, and the old cafeteria was replaced. Within two months, hourly workers enjoyed a new $800,000 cafeteria with the cheerful, upbeat feel of a fast-food restaurant.

"We just took the decision and did it," one manager commented.

Before Penske came aboard, Detroit Diesel's market share languished at around 3 percent of the heavy duty market. That share rose to 25 percent within three years. The beauty in this success is that the company relied almost entirely on the same blue-collar staff that Penske inherited when he took over in 1988. The company now competes head-to-head against Caterpillar and Cummins and posted sales of $2.3 billion in 1998.

Detroit Diesel can be found at **www.detroitdiesel.com**

What Roger Penske demonstrated at Detroit Diesel was exactly the kind of sensitivity which the new management of a merged company needs to show. It was no secret that employee motivation was low at Detroit Diesel and that it was probably one of the main contributors to low productivity. This directed Penske to look for something positive and quick which would help him earn buy-in from this particular group. This situational or contextual aspect cannot be overlooked and is the key to successfully identifying areas for early wins.

Where does this sensitivity come from? In the case of a major corporate merger, the sensitivity is largely a function of how well, how thoroughly, and how broadly you performed your due diligence. These facts and assumptions form the basis of your contextual knowledge of the merged company and allow you to zero in on exactly those areas where you need to achieve buy-in. Experience in other mergers or in restructuring efforts can also play a role.

Another example of an early win inside the company is the simplification or streamlining of decision making. French automaker Renault SA undertook such moves after investing in Japan's Nissan Motor and Nissan Diesel. Renault's relationship with Nissan does not involve a complete acquisition or merger. Renault, in fact, currently holds only minority stakes in the two Nissan units. But the transactions amount to a *de facto* takeover because of the influence Renault is expected to wield.

Renault and Nissan

Improvements in decision-making processes can take many forms. One method is to make decision teams smaller for the sake of speed and improved oversight. This is exactly what the French automaker Renault did shortly after investing $5.44 billion for a 37 percent stake in Japanese automaker Nissan Motor and a 23 percent stake in Nissan Diesel in March 1999.

In a management shake-up just three weeks later, Nissan announced it would reduce the size of its board of directors to ten members from 37. The move was attributed to the need to streamline its management structure and enhance super-vision of operations. Renault will have three seats on the board. One of those seats will be taken by Renault's "cost killer" and Executive Vice President Carlos Ghosn, who has also been named Nissan's COO.

Renault's Chairman Louis Schweitzer and his team remain under pressure to turn around Nissan's struggling operations by eliminating bloat and then generating growth. In the short-term, progress could be achieved via improved sourcing and the mutual sharing of knowledge assets such as R&D, manufacturing know-how and proprietary platforms. Over the long-term, Renault hopes to reduce Nissan's number of basic platforms to just ten from the current 34.

Geographically, the allied companies complement each other well. Renault has little presence in Japan and North America, two markets where Nissan is well-established.

Renault can be found at **www.renault.com**
Nissan can be found at **www.nissan-usa.com**

The benefits of shifting to positive areas – whether internal or external – should be clear, whether you are looking for early wins in terms of costs, sales, or knowledge. By focusing too heavily on the cost-savings story, you risk falling into a down-sizing spiral which is counterproductive. Job cuts could technically be defined as early wins from certain perspectives, but they can rapidly backfire and become "early losses" in terms of employee buy-in and orientation if they are not communicated quickly and defended in clear and fair terms.

> By focusing too heavily on the cost-savings story, you risk falling into a downsizing spiral which is counterproductive.

Look for early wins in assets, customers, and knowledge

When sufficient sensitivity has been gained as a result of proper due dili-gence, the list of places to achieve early wins on the cost side is limited only by your creativity and aggressiveness. The due diligence process will probably have revealed a long list of assets which are not essential to the operation of your company. It could be planes, helicopters, hotel suites, apartments, or limousines. Sell them. Fast.

Moving into the external area, there are also opportunities to reduce sourcing costs while improving relations with certain key suppliers. This opportunity should likewise not be underestimated. By developing spending estimates per sourcing group and profiling the most important sourcing groups, you build a basis for developing an overall savings estimate for your company. This leads to a business case and consequently a ramp-up plan which will help you save about 10 percent in third-party spending, if not more.

Sourcing can be a major source of efficiency synergies

Purchased materials, parts, components, systems and services account for up to 80 percent of company expenditures, depending on their degree of vertical integration. Therefore, a solid approach to sourcing is a major source of value creation. Procurement integration programs during PMI lead to major benefits by unlocking that potential for value creation.

The source of this potential is at least twofold: first, both partners profit from consolidation of many direct and indirect materials. This consolidated volume is considered a major synergy lever. Second, improvement effects will be achieved by streamlining the two procurement functions.

In a recent merger of two European utilities, a major source of value was captured through procurement integration. Savings of $60 million – representing a 12 percent reduction in costs – were realized. The success was built on strong CEO commitment and board support to foster organizational integration, cross-functional learning, a review of specification standards, and long-term contract renegotiations.

Procurement "engineering" in the course of a merger involves two major actions:

■ move procurement beyond cost cutting and make it a provider of strategic advantage – you can do this by leveraging supplier innovation potential and market developments, by restructuring, and by building a world-class supply base;

- upgrade the relatively low status of the traditional purchasing organization "silos" dramatically; establish cross-functional teams with high-caliber senior managers who can foster and achieve aggressive changes as well as hit cost saving targets.

A major global contractor was established based on the merger of four national and international contractors with combined global sales of around $2.5 billion and operations on five continents. The integration of global procurement has led to the setting up of an innovative "procurement business unit" with service and trading capabilities. It has already achieved savings in the range of 10 to 15 percent for major categories with a global supply base.

To take advantage of the opportunities offered by post-merger sourcing, we recommended the following steps:

- move quickly, do not hesitate, and make a compelling case for change;

- establish a new procurement organization up front with clear roles and responsibilities;

- define clear targets and decide how and in what time frame they should be measured using "hard" facts;

- challenge the status quo, with its long decision-making times and unnecessary need for consensus;

- avoid focusing only on short-term cost objectives;

- properly assess IT requirements and process issues;

- allocate sufficient resources;

- design steps to achieve a world-class procurement organization (ie from an organizational "silo" structure to the logic of a business unit).

Early wins by definition also have to come quickly. One particularly difficult place to achieve inward-looking early wins is in information technology. Much like the cultures of two merging companies, IT systems sometimes repel each other. In the worst cases, the systems are fundamentally incompatible and result in time-consuming switchovers or in lowest-common-denominator compromises.

If wins ever appear, they are anything but early. We saw in the case of Wells Fargo and First Interstate Bank that letting the future of a merger rise or fall on the immediate outcome of an IT renewal can worsen exactly what the renewal was supposed to improve: customer service.

This type of problem is not exclusive to IT integration. It can happen anywhere that two complex systems or processes are central to the operation of the business and need to be integrated. A railroad network, for instance, is such a system.

When Union Pacific and Southern Pacific Rail Corp merged in 1996 in a $3.9 billion deal, they combined to form what was then the largest US rail company. Management showed some good intentions at the outset, when it suggested that in addition to trying to save costs, the company would also focus on improving customer service.

Union Pacific and Southern Pacific Rail Corp

Union Pacific expected cost savings in the amount of $500 million as well as improvements in customer service when it merged with Southern Pacific Rail Corp in 1996 to form the largest railroad in the United States. Size, coverage, and cost are especially important factors in an industry where competition comes not only from other railroads, but also from trucks and ships.

The company, however, underestimated the effects that fierce competition from trucking had had on Southern Pacific. Its losses and relative inefficiencies meant that, despite any good intentions, any improvements would only be achievable over the long term. The integration of the two companies' IT systems – considered a major key to the merger – took over two years to complete.

The short-term effects, meanwhile, came early, and there were no wins among them. The new company could not cope with the increased freight volumes. Thousands of containers could not be shipped because freight cars were not available. Between 1996 and 1998, revenues for the combined railroad fell by 7 percent and carloadings by 9 percent, while operating income sank by 74 percent.

Union Pacific expects to finally complete the integration of Southern Pacific in 1999. The company's share price has risen by over 30 percent since summer 1998. Nonetheless, it remains only marginally above its level although the merger with Southern Pacific was consummated in September 1996.

Union Pacific can be found at **www.uprr.com**

Early wins are not called early wins for nothing. The underlying point – as in the section on "Leadership" – is that positive results need to come quickly. Mergers cannot be set aside for action or follow-up at a later date. This leads to drift. As the example of BMW and Rover shows, drift can get out of control if you leave it unchecked for too long. The German maker of high-end automobiles wanted to expand both upwards and outwards in the automotive market. It spent $2.1 billion to buy the 80 percent stake which British Aerospace held in Rover.

BMW and Rover

BMW wanted to enter the profitable off-road market with the Land Rover and expand its "low-end" segment in 1994. It was undisputed from the very beginning that Rover would remain an independent entity with its British character preserved. The fear of major changes finally triggered a dispute within the Rover management. John Towers moved from Managing Director to Chairman after George Simpson – who had initiated and carried out the deal on the British side – left the company right before the deal closed.

His appointment demonstrated that Rover would remain British and independent. Though this could fit the definition of an "early win" because it helped foster buy-in among the British employees, the move turned out to be a Trojan Horse.

Towers was the only member of the Rover management who had always strongly opposed the acquisition by BMW. Changes occurred slowly at Rover, and Towers was not replaced until 1996. By late 1998 – thanks in part to the delays in making needed restructurings – Rover was dragging down BMW's profitability. BMW Chairman Bernd Pieschetsrieder, a strong advocate of the Rover deal, was replaced in early 1999.

BMW can be found at **www.bmw.com**

The cases of Union Pacific and BMW show that good intentions and a focus on long-term or grander goals do not necessarily lead to or guarantee early wins. Nor does shifting the focus away from job cuts automatically lead to an increase in buy-in and goodwill.

Knowledge should not be neglected as a source of early wins. A company which has a solid track record in quick knowledge integration is the French automotive parts supplier Valeo SA. The company is extremely focused and has been highly successful in acquiring companies which can easily be integrated into its narrow – but growing and profitable – area of operation.

Valeo SA

An example of a company that emphasizes knowledge sharing and R&D integration quickly in the post-merger integration phase is the vehicle component system manufacturer Valeo SA. Much like a company such as Cisco Systems, Valeo is under high pressure to innovate rapidly and continue to differentiate itself.

Valeo's success in integrating new companies and their new products depends on ongoing interactions among R&D engineers, who meet regularly to exchange information and expertise across the various product lines. This experience and ability to integrate quickly has helped Valeo bring many companies into its fold over the past five years, by integrating acquired companies quickly into its information flow. Examples of tangible results include shared electronics systems across its modules, and clutch systems developed jointly by its Clutch and Friction Materials groups.

Because the company concentrates on vehicles and nothing else, its customer base is twofold. First, it includes major original equipment manufacturers (OEMs) which face similar issues such as innovation, continuous cost reduction, globalization and the shift from components to integrated systems. The number of such OEMs is diminishing because of the industry's current consolidation. Second, it includes a variety of after-market customers such as distributors and service providers.

Between 1993 and 1998, Valeo's revenues rose by 95 percent and its net income by 141 percent. The group now comprises 111 plants and 29 research facilities in 20 countries.

Valeo can be found at **www.valeo.com**

When you think of a knowledge industry in today's business world, an oil and gas company wouldn't come to mind immediately. But the merger of Exxon and Mobil is another example where rapid dissemination of shared knowledge will be crucial to success.

Exxon Mobil

Exxon and Mobil have promised to pursue short-term efficiency synergies as well as long-term growth opportunities. Upon completion of its merger, the company plans to aim for early wins in at least two areas: knowledge sharing and sourcing. Improvements in these areas and in exploration efficiency are expected to account for almost $900 million in savings.

Combining companies of this scale and scope creates opportunities for Exxon and Mobil to share best practices in areas such as refining, exploration, logistics, inventory handling, and raw materials procurement. But best practices represent only one aspect of knowledge sharing. The success of many of the planned growth opportunities will depend on how rapidly and efficiently the two companies can share their proprietary knowledge. Until now, each company has enjoyed proprietary patented technologies, which are, in many cases, complementary.

Despite anti-trust restrictions which preclude the companies from sharing too much information prior to regulatory approval, the effort to pinpoint precise areas for short-term or early wins has already begun. The company began its comprehensive due diligence process – encompassing legal, business, accounting and financial areas – in late 1998.

Exxon can be found at **www.exxon.com**
Mobil can be found at **www.mobil.com**

Cisco Systems, in contrast, works in an archetypal knowledge industry. Making acquisitions is one means by which the company preserves its leading technological edge as well as its 80 percent market share in Internet routers. Some of the equipment or expertise which Cisco feels it requires may have taken more resources – either in time, money, or personnel – to develop internally. The rapid integration of knowledge assets is thus not only a priority in the post-merger integration phase. It is often the driving force behind the acquisition decision.

Look for substantial, sustainable, and tangible results

The trickiest part of achieving an early win is the magnitude. If you shoot for something too large, it might take too long to achieve anything substantial or positive which can be communicated as an early win. Trivial moves, meanwhile, can lead to the impression that management has taken its eye off the most important, crucial issues. We see no problem, however, if companies pursue low-hanging fruit in order to achieve early wins. The risk that your move will be seen as trivial is much lower than the risk of failure if you pursue a target which turns out to be too much to handle.

Within the context of this book, it would be impossible to offer a definitive answer or strict methodology aimed at getting the size of your early win "just right." Doing this depends on the unique situation of the companies involved. This prevents us from making blanket generalizations. Nonetheless, an early win must fulfill the following two criteria.

■ Early wins must be results-driven in order to ensure credibility. As we mentioned at the outset, it is time for action. The merged company needs to say what it has accomplished, not what it has planned or what it has launched.

■ Early wins must be clear to everybody. They must be tangible, and they must be simple and easy to understand. Such wins are easier to publicize, especially when they are surprising. This is an open invitation to slaughter the sacred cows, attack the bloat of paperwork and forms, and share benefits more broadly.

> Early wins must be clear to everybody. They must be tangible, and they must be simple and easy to understand.

Gather information by asking and listening

Like many of the other guidelines discussed in this book, the main problem is not that the rules and the necessary steps are complicated and involving. Rather, the problem lies in inaction. Nothing is done, or what is done is too little and too late.

There are startlingly simple ways to begin to gather information and find out what constituencies expect in terms of early wins, in what magnitude and on what timetable. The easiest method of all is to ask them.

This mirrors once again the example of Roger Penske and the cafeteria at the Detroit Diesel factory. Knowing that the problem of low productivity might lie with employee motivation, he went directly to the source and gathered information on his own.

You do not necessarily need to conduct such interviews face-to-face. In many cases, with the current magnitude of mergers worldwide, it is literally impossible for, say, Boeing Chairman Phil Condit to interview 60,000 employees from McDonnell Douglas, plus around 220,000 Boeing employees.

It is possible, however, to do selective interviews, to use modern media such as e-mail, or to conduct quick, down-and-dirty surveys. Ask the 120,000 employees in the organization how a particular goal could be realized. Ask them to tell you what three things management should undertake immediately. Float trial balloons and ask the employees what they think.

This process itself – independent of the results – addresses the three key elements which are necessary to achieve buy-in: information, involvement, and communication.

The contact between management and the individual stakeholder group is an opportunity to provide additional information, tailored to address whatever perceptual problem or challenge the merger may have generated. The dialogue gives the stakeholder a sense of involvement, much like a vote or an indirect "say" in how the merger can move forward positively and productively. Finally, the communication of a substantial and sustainable result reinforces this feeling of involvement. It demonstrates that the move to reach out to the stakeholder was not a cosmetic, smoke-and-mirrors trick which was meant to deceive or to throw someone off guard.

Get the word out, but don't exaggerate

One of the common threads through the whole post-merger integration process is the striking of a balance between setting an orientation, achieving buy-in, and managing expectations. This dynamic holds true for the communication of early wins.

Even if you have hit the shop floor, done the due diligence, and achieved somthing which would qualify as an early win, the work is not yet over with. The early win should be trumpeted. Proclaim it simply and clearly through as many media as possible. This area will be discussed in more detail in "Rule 6: Communication."

Striking this balance depends strongly on the situation and your sensitivity to it. But in any event, you must make sure that the thrust of the communication is a completed task. This could be the closure of one phase of a longer-term project, or the completion of a small act in its entirety.

The risk of a misunderstanding or misinterpretation increases as you focus on communicating that a plan has been made and launched. This communication is not concrete enough. If you recall the scenario with which we began this chapter, you can imagine how tough a sell you would have if you responded by saying we are launching a plan. It could work, but in these cases nothing sells like a positive, motivating act which your stakeholders can instantly relate to.

> Nothing sells like a positive, motivating act which your stakeholders can instantly relate to.

The new rule for "early wins" is simple:
act, get results, and communicate – make tangible, positive moves.

The urgency is high, but the levers for making a positive move are every-where. Make sure that you achieve at least one early win within the first 30 days after the merger. This is only possible if you use your common sense, take a critical look at your situation, and then act. Low-hanging fruit can buy some credibility, but long-term projects with a grand scale will take too long for your impatient stakeholders. Substantial and sus-tainable deeds – especially those which are driven by broad-based involvement – are sure-fire early wins. Finally, you need to get the word out as quickly as possible, but without exaggerating.

What you have to do

- **Do your due diligence.** You can only get early wins if you have done your due diligence properly.

- **Design early wins according to the buy-in needs.** You need the sensi-tivity to know what you need and what your situation is, to iden-tify more precisely where you should look and to determine how substantial a move you must make. In this case, it is better to err on the side of something small and manageable.

- **Look internally, but above all look externally.** Early wins in outward-looking areas such as customers and suppliers can have a high impact, but are often neglected at the expense of internally-focused early wins.

- **Focus on assets, customers, and knowledge.** These are rich sources of early wins.

- **Get cost-cutting out of the way** as quickly as possible, but do not sell these as early wins.

- **Gather information by asking and listening.** This gets your con-stituencies involved.

- **Communicate completed tasks quickly,** but without exaggerating.

RULE 5

Cultural differences

*Handle a "soft" issue with
"hard" measures*

Summary

"Cultural differences" are the most frequently quoted reason for failure in mergers and acquisitions, both before and after the deal is done. However, culture is often used as a catch-all covering behaviors, objectives, self-interest and ego, and any other reasons people do not want to discuss openly.

Cultural integration is critical to the success of any merger. It can be managed as a defined process, provided that it is approached in a structured way.

In our survey of 115 transactions around the world, we discovered one fact that points to why many mergers are unsuccessful and why "cultural differences" are blamed.

✳ **Fact: cultural imposition is the norm.**
Whether or not this is the most appropriate strategy for cultural integration.

While imposing one culture on another is valid in some cases, it can destroy the value the merger was supposed to create if it is applied without thought, or implemented badly.

In particular, where the two organizations serve very different markets, it is often best to leave the cultures separate and intact. Where the two organizations need to be fully integrated to release value, then a "compound" culture should be created, taking the best elements from each of the parent organizations to create a culturally superior child.

Today you have your first meeting with selected managers and department heads of the company you have decided to buy. It is the first time you have been in Northern California, and now you are headed to their office.

You keep reminding yourself that the gentlemen you will be meeting this morning at 9.30 a.m. are not the same ones you actually struck the deal with. They don't sail yachts from Newport, Rhode Island, and they weren't at the latest World Economic Forum in Davos, Switzerland.

All you can hear as you enter the meeting room are the last few casual remarks of your chief financial officer, as if he were standing right next to you. "Come on," he said. "It's not like we're buying Samsung or Siemens. They're just like us. Same country. Same language. How different can they be?"

That's exactly the question. How different can they be? These words pop into your head at least a hundred times as you scan the layout of the room. There is no horseshoe arrangement of tables with an overhead projector at the front. Rather, there are tables of various sizes scattered throughout the room, and a beamer for multimedia presentations in the center. All seats – except, of course, those for your team – have a state-of-the-art laptop at them, hooked up to the beamer. How will you show the slides you prepared?

There is no paper. No flip charts. There is also no coffee. In fact, there is nothing to eat or drink at all. The few members of the "other side" who have entered likewise stand out. They shift enormous paper Starbucks coffee cups from their right hands to the left, shake your hand, and say "Hi, you're Bill, right? How you doing?"

In contrast to your team, none of them are wearing suits, but at least half are wearing earrings.

As you stand there for what seems like an eternity, you begin wondering whether it really was a good idea to rent the limousine for the ride in from the airport. Then it suddenly occurs to you that it is now 9.37 a.m. The meeting should have already begun.

"Hey, Bill, don't sweat it. Our guys will be here in a couple of minutes. Just make yourself at home."

The final question in your mind, when the meeting ultimately begins, is not "How different can they be?" but rather, "How in the world are we going to ever work with these people?"

Overcoming cultural differences is by far the most troublesome aspect of making mergers and acquisitions work. People from different cultures are suddenly thrust together and expected to address complex issues of strategy and working practices. The situation is made worse by uncertainty over who will get what job, what will get divested, and exactly how the "synergistic cost reductions" will be achieved.

The situation is made more difficult when different nationalities are involved. The global mergers trend was examined in the German newsweekly *Der Spiegel* in a lengthy article late in 1998 under the title "Welt AG," which translates roughly as "World Inc." The article used the current merger integration efforts at DaimlerChrysler to discuss a futuristic world filled with virtual countries and virtual companies. In this world, top managers – using English as the world's *lingua franca*, regardless of where they are from – lose their links to their home country in a melting pot on a worldwide scale. This level of global integration will clearly require companies to be able to integrate people with widely differing cultures and expectations far more successfully than most manage today.

It is the very pervasiveness of culture, and the difficulty of defining exactly what it is, that leads to its being blamed for so many merger failures. "Cultural differences" are used as a catch-all to encompass failures in communication, divergence of objectives, differences in business models, political rivalries, and clashes of ego.

In order to manage cultural issues, culture itself must be defined, issues must be articulated, and practical strategies implemented. Without putting these in place, no merger or acquisition can be guaranteed to succeed.

So, what is culture anyway?

There are many definitions of what culture is, and how it works. Sociologists, anthropologists, psychologists and management scientists all have their definitions from their own particular perspectives.

Practically, the culture of a company is the set of assumptions, beliefs and accepted "rules" of conduct that define "how things work around here." These assumptions, beliefs and rules are not written down, and indeed most people in an organization would be hard pressed to articulate what they are. But knowing the rules, and sharing the beliefs, defines "us," and anyone who does not follow the rules is immediately classified as "them."

What is the purpose of culture? The culture of an organization is extremely important for its effective functioning. Every individual is different, each with his or her own experiences, beliefs and capabilities. Large global companies may encompass dozens of nationalities and people with a huge spectrum of backgrounds. Organizational culture provides a common medium and language that allows people to communicate, to work together in teams, and to perform tasks. It provides the rules of response to uncertainty. Socially, it provides a sense of belonging and the social interaction that all humans require. Politically, it provides the rules by which people can pursue their legitimate self-interest.

How does culture develop? Culture is created by the people within an organization, and more especially by the leaders. Culture creation starts with the founder or builder. Walk into a McDonald's restaurant in the United States, and you will usually see a bronze plaque next to the counter with a relief of McDonald's visionary Ray Kroc. The text on the plaque underscores Kroc's vision and his contribution to building the fast-food empire. The hallmark of the advertising agency Leo Burnett, meanwhile, was the bowl of apples which you would find on every reception desk in every office. This bowl was a subtle reminder of the man who founded the firm during the Great Depression and had a bowl of apples served on the table at his fledgling agency's very first meeting.

New layers of culture are added with each new generation of leadership. Employees and managers tend to follow the example of their current leaders. By their actions and words, leaders demonstrate new beliefs, new assumptions, new priorities and new rules of behavior that will be added to historical precedent. Employees will look to see how their leaders respond to new threats, and if successful, will copy their responses. They will look to see who succeeds in the organization, and will copy them in the hope that they too will be successful.

Organizational controls and processes are also important elements of "culture." A cultural "currency" of pay, reward, sanctions, job titles, measures, symbols of power and status is created to reinforce the rules of acceptable behavior. A series of unspoken "contracts" grows up between the organization and the employee, which defines how employees will be rewarded if they follow the rules. For example, the social contract in Japan has historically been quite different from that in the West. When the Japanese "contract" of lifetime employment in return for loyalty is broken, and people are made redundant, feelings of betrayal and shame can result. Compare this to many industries in Anglo-Saxon countries, when being made redundant is increasingly seen as an occupational hazard, likely to be experienced by most people at some time or another in their careers.

> A series of unspoken "contracts" grows up between the organization and the employee, which defines how employees will be rewarded if they follow the rules.

The culture of the company is critically important to its success. A strong culture that is well-suited to the business environment of the day will bring assured success. Jack Welch of General Electric has, through his actions, created a culture that is almost perfectly matched to the *zeitgeist* of the 1990s, and the company has been incredibly successful in virtually all its endeavors. It is said that the British Empire, the most geographically successful organization the world has ever known, was formed "on the playing fields of Eton." The beliefs and rules of conduct drilled into young boys at British public schools in turn created colonial administrations throughout five continents.

However, while strong cultures can be world-beaters, when the world changes, they must change also, and the stronger the culture, the more difficult it is to change. The same culture that took IBM to world dominance nearly destroyed it when the availability of cheap and powerful personal computers destroyed the value of the franchise that it had so carefully built within the corporate board room.

Throughout the world, companies are struggling to change their cultures to meet the new realities of business. But changing culture is immensely difficult. It requires consistent and symbolic demonstration by leadership of the new rules and priorities, constant communication, and reinforcement. It requires wholesale replacement of the cultural "currency" of systems, procedures, and symbols. It also requires persistence, as the process is not only hard, but can take many years to achieve.

Getting it wrong can destroy the value of a merger

Communication between different cultures is always difficult, as the culture of a company is a very specific language. The British and Americans have been described as "two cultures divided by a common language." Although the words are often the same, the meaning and unspoken assumptions can be very different, leading to misunderstanding and confusion.

However, culture is as much a value driver of a company as its assets, products, customers, and even the individual capabilities of its people. Any company acquiring another should be very clear about what it wishes to do with this cultural asset, and how to maximize its value. Dealing with cultural issues inappropriately can destroy much of the value that the deal was supposed to create.

The most common way of dealing with cultural mismatches is for one culture to impose itself on another. A telling example of the downside of this approach is the merger of Homedco Group and Abbey Healthcare in the summer of 1995. The merger resulted in the largest provider and manager of integrated home care products and services in the United States. The managers on both sides had hoped both for economies of scale and an expanded geographical reach.

Apria Healthcare Group Inc

The merger between Abbey Healthcare Group and Homedco Group in 1995 turned out to be more complicated than expected. The planned merger of equals increasingly took on the features of an acquisition, with many Abbey managers leaving the company.

The management problems masked a deeper underlying problem: cultural differences. Homedco's conservative management style with stringent controls and thick bureaucracy clashed with the dynamic business style at Abbey, characterized by a lean management with far-reaching delegation of responsibilities.

IT is a powerful element of the cultural system, and the companies clashed in this arena as well. The decision to adopt Abbey's computer system as the overall company system resulted in order backlogs, partly because Homedco managers were not familiar with the system. In 1996, the accounts receivable rose significantly because the customers' willingness to pay deteriorated.

In the midst of its integration difficulties, Apria also missed an opportunity to make early wins. On the customer side, it had a wide opportunity to focus on smaller physicians and hospitals and to build up its business there. These customers would have provided wider profit margins, but Apria opted to pursue contracts with big healthcare providers, where margins are smaller.

Apria's share price fell from $32.50 in early 1996 to as low as $2.50 in 1998, before recovering to above $22 per share in June 1999.

Apria Healthcare can be found at **www.apria.com**

Another case where one culture was imposed on another with disastrous consequences occurred in 1987, when the profitable and successful regional airline USAir purchased another profitable and successful regional airline, Piedmont Aviation, in the largest airline merger ever. The similarities between the two companies stopped, however, at "profitable" and "successful," and even these words no longer applied two years later. The combined company had swung to a loss. While much of the airline industry also experienced a downturn at this time, USAir's woes were not cyclical, but rather self-inflicted.

USAir

Despite obvious cultural differences, when the Pittsburgh-based USAir bought Piedmont, a leading regional carrier in the southern and eastern US, for $1.6 billion in 1987, it immediately attempted to impose its own culture onto Piedmont's.

When USAir attempted what appeared, to it, to be minor changes in service – such as the elimination of baskets of cookies and granola bars on short flights – the result was an immediate and harsh backlash from regular Piedmont customers. But differences in customer orientation were only one example of the cultural differences. USAir had the entrenched, bureaucratic feel of a dominant yet complacent company, while Piedmont exhibited a more entrepreneurial spirit which had fostered a high level of workforce commitment. The differences showed up in everything, from how they processed passengers to how they paid their pilots.

The internal and external problems became so severe that the integration of the airlines can be summed up in two sets of figures: by August 1990, USAir's share price had plummeted to $16.25 per share from $54.75 one year earlier. Furthermore, the airline had an on-time arrivals rate of just 68.4 percent, almost eight percentage points below the industry average and 17 points below then-leader American Airlines.

The losses for the once profitable and stable airline became so severe that the company neared bankruptcy and saw its credit rating lowered by Moody's due to cash flow problems.

USAir returned to profitability in 1995 and changed its name to US Airways in 1997. It now ranks as the fifth-largest passenger airline in the world.

US Airways can be found at **www.usairways.com**

Concerns about cultural imposition may cause the deal to fail even before it starts.

Sega and Bandai

In January 1997, Japanese video game maker Sega Enterprises Ltd agreed to acquire Japan's largest toy company, Bandai Co in a deal worth over $1 billion with the objective of becoming a global entertainment company second only to Walt Disney.

Within three months, the deal was in trouble. The cultures of the companies were very different. Sega was an entrepreneurial company that started as an American firm serving US occupation forces in Japan, and Bandai was run along far more traditional Japanese lines. As a result, over 80 percent of Bandai's middle management expressed concern about the merger, fearing for their jobs and that Bandai would lose its corporate identity.

By the end of May, the deal was dead, and Bandai admitted that it had been unable to identify synergies between the companies. By the end of June, Bandai's CEO, six other directors, and two auditors, had all resigned.

Sega can be found at **www.sega.com** or **www.sega.co.ip**
Bandai can be found at **www.bandai.com**

As in the case of Sega and Bandai, "culture" is often a euphemism for politics and self-interest. Probably the highest profile example of "culture" destroying a deal that may well have created enormous value was the much-publicized case of the not-quite merger of GlaxoWellcome and SmithKline Beecham in 1998.

GlaxoWellcome and SmithKline Beecham

The "merger of equals" between GlaxoWellcome and SmithKline Beecham was hailed by analysts as an almost perfect fit. With strong, but complementary, product ranges, the merger would have created the world's largest pharmaceutical company with efficiency synergies in excess of $1.5 billion and a research budget of $3 billion a year.

However, within a month, the deal had collapsed, with SmithKlein Beecham accusing GlaxoWellcome of reneging on agreements, and irreconcilable differences in "approaches to the merger, management philosophy, and corporate culture."

The crux of the matter, it emerged, was an argument about who got what job on the board of the new company. The original agreement was that GlaxoWellcome would have three of the five seats, and SmithKline Beecham two, a ratio decided on the basis of the relative market capitalization.

This particular clash of egos destroyed $21 billion worth of potential shareholder value.

GlaxoWellcome can be found at **www.glaxowellcome.com**
SmithKline Beecham can be found at **www.sb.com**

Getting the approach right: three basic options

There are many strategies for dealing with cultural issues after a merger or acquisition, and you must choose your approach carefully, having understood the consequences. The only strategy that is always wrong is to ignore the problem.

There are three basic strategies: one culture can be imposed on another, the cultures can be left separate or allowed to merge over an extended time, or a "compound" culture can be created, taking the best "genes" from each parent to create a better child.

Deciding which approach to adopt will depend on a number of different factors: the reasons for the original transaction, relative size and strengths of the businesses, the overlap of market proposition, and the similarity of the cultures.

Cultural imposition

Cultural imposition is the norm. While, as in the case of USAir and Apria this can destroy value, if executed well and for the right reasons, it can be the most appropriate approach.

Hanson Trust

Lords Hanson and White developed a formula that allowed them to build a $17 billion conglomerate, delivering exceptional value to shareholders. For over three decades they acquired dozens of companies in low tech, commodities type industries, and managed them for cash flow and shareholder value.

The hallmark of their operation was ruthless elimination of unnecessary overheads, and rapid imposition of strict and well-honed financial controls.

Lord Hanson's dictum that "the shareholder is king" finally led him to break up the group in 1996.

In the case of Hanson Trust, the whole premise of the transaction was the replacement of bloated bureaucracy with a strong, lean, controlling culture more appropriate for the commodity markets that the acquired companies served.

3M is another company with a strong culture and some successful acquisitions. However, the rationale, and the approach, is quite different. 3M's great cultural strength is its ability to innovate. It grows in part by identifying small companies with great ideas, nurturing their creativity, but providing the necessary expertise and infrastructure to develop the products and bring them to market.

While not strictly M&A, possibly the ultimate example of serial and successful cultural imposition is information technology (IT) outsourcing. Here, a specialist IT company takes over the IT infrastructure and departments of large companies and, through improvements in efficiency and delivery, supplies more up-to-date services at lower cost.

US-based Electronic Data Systems (EDS) invented the concept. Its ability to impose a culture quickly and without trauma is a core element of its business. The rationale for introducing a new culture is strong. As an IT company, it has a culture which is generally more suited to IT service delivery than any in-house IT department. One of the selling points to the people who move across is the opportunity to grow professionally and move elsewhere in EDS. It is therefore critical that the new employees are "transitioned" from the old to the new culture as quickly as possible.

Electronic Data Systems (EDS)

Since its formation in 1962, EDS has grown into an organization of over 100,000 employees. Around a third of its employees have been absorbed through over 400 outsourcing deals from industries as diverse as healthcare and aerospace. In their European operations, over 70 percent have come through transitions from other companies.

Merging people of such diverse backgrounds into a single cultural model is a core capability of EDS. As soon as an outsourcing deal is signed, a well-practiced transitioning process snaps into action. Experienced "EDSers" take on leadership roles. Human resource specialists are brought in to explain to every employee how the transition will take place, what is expected of them, the new procedures and terms of employment, and the benefits of being part of EDS. People who have transitioned to EDS in the past are made available to discuss fears and concerns. Communication, retraining and support programs are put in place, and all employees are helped to make their own decision about their future in the new organization.

Five years after joining, 70 percent of transitioned employees in the US are still with the firm, no mean feat in the IT industry.

EDS can be found at **www.eds.com**

In looking at these examples there are clear success factors. First, there must be clear reasons for imposing the new culture, and the new culture must be demonstrably more appropriate to the business environment than the old one. The new culture must be imposed quickly, explicitly and completely. Second, the benefits of the new arrangement must be communicated effectively, and support systems must be put in place to help people to adapt to the new situation. New leadership must be put in place that consistently demonstrates the new norms of behavior. A new "cultural currency" of organizational systems and symbols must be put in place quickly. New expectations must be clearly communicated, and people given the choice to stay or go. Above all, there must be no cultural limbo. Decisive action is the kindest route forward.

> There must be clear reasons for imposing the new culture, and the new culture must be demonstrably more appropriate to the business environment than the old one.

Allowing cultures to remain separate

A culture that is successful in one market will not necessarily work in another. Where the merger or acquisition is between businesses in quite different sectors, then often their cultures should be left separate.

This was the rationale for the approach used in the acquisition of US-based publisher Ziff Davis by Japan's Softbank, the dominant software distributor in Japan.

Softbank is more than just a software wholesaler. It resembles rather a visionary movement launched by Korean-born and American-educated Masayoshi Son, a 40-year-old entrepreneur who is sometimes called the Bill Gates of Japan. As Chief Executive of Softbank, he has the goal of becoming the "premier provider of infrastructure to the personal computer industry." This explains his motivation to buy stakes in major companies involved in spreading the digital theology. It led him to buy Ziff Davis, which dominates the US market for PC-related magazines, in two phases, and likewise to buy the rights to the Comdex trade fair, the major US trade show for computer technology. Market observers raised doubts, however, about Son's ability to manage his growing collection of American companies and interests, which include links to Novell and Cisco, among others.

> Where the merger or acquisition is between businesses in quite different sectors, then often their cultures should be left separate.

Softbank and Ziff Davis

Masayoshi Son's reputation for having an "American" way of doing business has helped him attract US partners. But Son actually considers himself a person who is not really typically Japanese, American or Korean. He attributes his knowledge of entrepreneurship to his education in the United States and claims it gave him a good understanding of American culture.

At the time of the Ziff Davis acquisition in 1995, it was unprecedented for a Japanese concern to own a major American publisher. The question was whether Japanese editorial practices – where it is not unusual for certain companies to receive special play – could carry over to US operations in a Japanese-owned publishing house. Under Japanese control, it was feared, the publisher could potentially pressure reporters to favor major exhibitors at its own trade shows.

To his credit, Son has said he saw no need to make changes in the management or operation of the businesses he acquired. Editors at Ziff Davis have also remarked that they have retained editorial control.

By 1999 Softbank had consolidated revenues of $4.4 billion.

Softbank can be found at **www.softbank.com**
Ziff Davis can be found at **www.zd.com**

Leaving cultures to operate separately clearly raises the question as to what the value of such acquisitions might be. Maintaining separate cultures inevitably reduces the possibility for communication, and makes synergistic benefits difficult to realize.

A variation on the approach is to allow the companies to grow together at their own pace. While less traumatic and risky than more assertive interventions to change culture, the process is slow, and so it is uncertain when, if ever, synergies will be realized.

Pacific Telesis and SBC Communications

The new telecommunications regulations in the United States resulted in increased competition in the industry. This new intensity has prompted many companies – both large and small – to seek competitive advantages through a merger.

The $16.5 billion merger between Pacific Telesis Group and SBC Communications in April 1996 was primarily driven by the need for growth and size. The constructive synergy opportunities for the new company, which had become the second-largest American telecommunications company behind AT&T, seemed substantial, thanks to the combination of strengths in local, long distance, international, and cellular service.

But the key to success lay in achieving a healthy mixture of the two companies' different management cultures. The "California–West Coast" stereotype which typified PacTel – reinforced by the influence of Silicon Valley and Stanford University – was set to collide with the more down-to-earth SBC culture from Texas, where the stereotype has more to do with barbecue than bits and bytes. The differences did not stop at stereotypes, however. PacTel had pursued a more cost-oriented strategy, while SBC had a reputation for being more market- and customer-driven.

The two companies prevented a lethal head-on collision by deciding to let the companies continue to operate for the time being as separate units, supported by a selected number of centralized functions. This decision was received positively, all the more because the new organization on balance created more jobs than it trimmed.

SBC can be found at **www.sbc.com**

Creating a compound culture

Possibly the most difficult, but ultimately most valuable, approach to resolving cultural differences is to create a "compound" culture, a new set of beliefs, assumptions and rules of behavior that exploit the strengths of both of the parent companies to create a new and better culture.

The whole rationale behind the merger of Daimler-Benz of Germany and Chrysler of the US demanded that the companies merge into a new entity. Despite hugely different histories, approaches, markets, remuneration systems and beliefs, a new integrated company must be created if the synergistic benefits are to be realized. Indeed, it was partly to pick up Chrysler's lean ways that Daimler entered into the merger.

DaimlerChrysler has begun to make headway in the area of cultural integration, in part by doing its homework. Shortly after the deal became public in early May 1998, two of the company's German competitors – Porsche and Audi – made pessimistic prognoses for the merger's future. The company would collapse under the weight of cultural differences, they argued.

This risk of cultural implosion was no secret to DaimlerChrysler, however, because Daimler-Benz performed an in-depth analysis of culture as a success factor prior to completing the negotiations with Chrysler.

DaimlerChrysler

Too much was at stake in this deal for the companies to accept conventional wisdom that the majority of mergers fail. They wanted confirmation, and they wanted to know why.

This led Daimler-Benz to conduct a study of large, cross-border mergers and joint ventures to examine their failure rate and the reasons why. Their work showed that more than 70 percent of parties in such transactions admit failure within three years. In a more detailed examination of 50 of those failures, the company repeatedly encountered cultural conflict as a problem. The DaimlerChrysler post-merger integration project was ultimately built around a list of a dozen or so major tasks, derived from a list of almost 100 potential pitfalls in the post-merger integration process.

The realism with which DaimlerChrysler has pursued integration on the cultural side is refreshing. The company plays up its cultural differences instead of hoping they will go away. It freely admits that it is impossible to make everybody happy. The company also wants to consciously avoid a balanced form of cherry-picking from each organization, instead preferring to try to compound the two cultures into something sustainable.

DaimlerChrysler can be found at **www.daimlerchrysler.com**

One of the key success factors in making a merger work is to put the new management team in place quickly. Whatever internal differences they may have, the leadership of the new company must outwardly appear to be unified, and must lead by example. While the leadership team should be taken from both parents, this should be on the basis of "the best people for the job," and with an eye to the new cultural model that the organization is trying to create.

ABC and Capital Cities

In 1986 Capital Cities, a company with assets of $1.2 billion, acquired the much larger American Broadcasting Corporation (ABC) for $3.5 billion in a deal that had all the hallmarks of a potential cultural battlefield.

While Capital Cities had a strong, textbook and cost-focused management style, ABC had a history of informality and generosity bordering on the profligate. Although ABC clearly needed the more focused management that the Capital Cities management team, led by Dan Burke and Tom Murphy, would bring, it was obviously not going to be easy. Capital Cities had no experience in running TV networks, and needed to exploit the ABC management team, but they also had to address the fundamental performance issues that were building up in ABC.

Burke and Murphy's experience of successfully completing over 30 acquisitions came to the fore. The period after the merger was difficult, with job losses and failing performance. However, despite tough action and many changes which ABC personnel found difficult, the situation was managed very successfully by the diplomatic duo. Clear strategic direction, a self-deprecating acknowledgement of the cultural differences between them, and clear delegation of responsibility for solving the problems to the existing ABC managers helped to turn the business around.

In 1996 Capital Cities/ABC was sold to the Disney Corporation for $19 billion.

Once the leadership is in place, it is critical to build communication channels between the two cultures. Buddy systems, joint teams, co-location and informal events are all tools that can help this interaction. A mutual respect must be established between the cultures of the two organizations. The objective is to understand what the most appropriate culture should be, and to build it from the elements available. Neither culture is being destroyed, rather both give parts of themselves to the future company.

Cultural compounding must start with an honest and thorough assessment of the two cultures, and the needs for the future. This will allow you to define areas which can be handled relatively swiftly, areas where friction may occur, and also the positive areas – situations where the companies show a strong similarity in orientation at a high level. Such situations offer the new organization an opportunity to capitalize on these strengths and create a powerful force to move the company forward.

A history of success in mergers is also a good indicator that the new merger will be successful. In our survey, three quarters of the most successful acquirers had completed three or more transactions in the previous five years.

> In our survey, three quarters of the most successful acquirers had completed three or more transactions in the previous five years.

A good case in point is the 1998 merger between the multinational oil giants British Petroleum (BP) and the US-based Amoco. BP feels that its international experience – especially its US experience in integrating Standard Oil of Ohio (Sohio) over the last ten years – will assist it greatly in making sure that the post-merger integration of Amoco will not be bogged down by cultural considerations. Amoco itself has made significant acquisitions in the last ten years, such as its purchase of Canada's Dome Petroleum in the 1980s.

BP Amoco

BP Chief Executive Sir John Browne, who will head the combined company, and BP Deputy Chief Executive Rodney Chase feel that BP and Amoco enjoy similar corporate cultures, which means that the merger should not be difficult to accomplish in cultural terms. The two companies have experience working throughout the world, from Asia to South America. Furthermore, BP has considerable experience in North American operations, first with its assistance in building the Alaska Pipeline, and then through its 1987 acquisition of Standard Oil of Ohio.

The new company would rank second only to Royal Dutch Shell in production, with a daily oil and natural gas output equivalent to 2.9 million barrels. A merger between Mobil and BP would have resulted in an even bigger company, but this idea was rejected precisely for cultural reasons. Chase said that during the previous merger talks with Mobil, it became clear that the companies' corporate cultures didn't fit well together. The two sides were unable to find a mutually satisfactory agreement, and the idea was dropped.

Experience in Amoco's market and in integrating a US company are only part of the reason BP feels it can combine the two cultures successfully. Browne himself has first-hand experience in seeing how cultural issues can be an asset or a wedge. As a director of Daimler-Benz, he saw the company's meticulous preparation of its merger with Chrysler. And as a board member of SmithKline Beecham, he saw how the failure to address cultural issues can scupper a merger before it even begins.

In the spring of 1999 reports began to emerge that the cultural integration had turned into more of an imposition of BP's culture on Amoco. This situation may be made more complicated by BP Amoco's decision in March to pursue the purchase of Atlantic Richfield (Arco) for an estimated $25 billion.

BP Amoco can be found at **www.bpamoco.com**

A consistent theme of successful acquirers is that they gain a realistic understanding of the cultural gap before they start, and are happy to walk away if the gap is too wide.

Making a cultural assessment

Assessment of culture is difficult, as so much is hidden, even to the people within the culture itself. Nevertheless, you should perform an initial cultural assessment very early on, and then a more thorough analysis after the deal has been done.

An honest and thorough assessment will allow you to define areas which can be handled relatively swiftly, areas where friction may occur, and also the positive areas – situations where the companies show a strong similarity in orientation at a high level. Such situations offer the new organization an opportunity to capitalize on these strengths and create a powerful new force to move the new company forward. Your task at that juncture is to facilitate interactions, not to dictate outcomes.

Having understood what differences must be bridged, and what the new organizational culture should be, you must then create a new "cultural currency" to support and nurture the new culture.

The name of the new organization is an important symbol of the new culture. On its own, a new name and a colorful logo are obviously not sufficient to bind several thousand employees – who just weeks before were probably bitter rivals – to a common cause and ask them to work

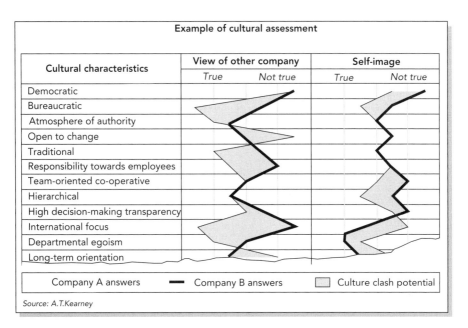

Example of cultural assessment

Cultural characteristics	View of other company		Self-image	
	True	Not true	True	Not true
Democratic				
Bureaucratic				
Atmosphere of authority				
Open to change				
Traditional				
Responsibility towards employees				
Team-oriented co-operative				
Hierarchical				
High decision-making transparency				
International focus				
Departmental egoism				
Long-term orientation				

Company A answers ▬ Company B answers ☐ Culture clash potential

Source: A.T.Kearney

Fig. 7 Cultural gaps reveal potential for culture clash

willingly toward a common goal. But its effective communication can make it a powerful signal that a new identity will be created.

Company one	Company two	Name of new company
Traveler's	Citicorp	Citigroup
Daimler-Benz	Chrysler	DaimlerChrysler
Grand Metropolitan	Guinness	Diageo
Hoechst	Rhone-Poulenc	Aventis
James River Corp.	Fort Howard	Fort James
Siebe plc	BTR plc	Invensys
Ciba-Geigy	Sandoz	Novartis
SmithKlineBeckman	Beecham	SmithKline Beecham
Union Bank of Switzerland	Swiss Bank Corporation	United Bank of Switzerland

Fig. 8 Some of the names adopted by mega-mergers

In the best of cases, the choice of a new name supports the vision for the newly-merged company. In this respect, the British engineering company Invensys is off to a good start.

Invensys

In March 1999, the merger partners in the $5 billion deal between Siebe plc and BTR plc decided to change the name of the combined company to Invensys. This erases the names of two old-line British engineering firms with well-known reputations. The new name, however, stands for innovation, invention, and systems work and embraces the company's vision to be a world leader in control systems by delivering complicated automation systems to the average household.

The company still faces the challenge of integrating two vastly different cultures. Siebe has emphasized just-in-time and boasted a flat hierarchy, while BTR is a more traditional manufacturing company with a more top-down management style.

To publicize the new name, the company has taken out full-page ads in leading business publications.

Invensys can be found at **www.invensys.com**

As important as the symbolism of a new name is the creation of the other elements of the new "cultural currency," the human resource systems and performance measures that must unite the new organizations. All this requires constant communication, a topic that is addressed in the next rule in detail.

If the decision has been taken to create a compound culture, special attention must be taken to avoid cultural repression by one party. "Safe haven" mentalities, where people cling – sometimes desperately, sometimes aggressively – to their old ways of doing things, must not be allowed to occur. A cultural void must be prevented, to avoid employees becoming mercenary and detached as the rituals and incentives they are accustomed to are taken away, with no prospect of something better.

The difficulty lies in having the patience and the persistence to monitor the process of cultural change. On the one hand, you want to avoid an environment whose philosophy is interpreted as "put up or shut up." On the other hand, a *laissez-faire* or hands-off approach to cultural compounding can degenerate into an unproductive battle of self-interest and turf wars. You need to strike a balance between these two opposing poles.

The new rule: cultural imposition is not always the option. It is often more suitable to "compound" the cultures or even let them remain separate.

Value creation will be maximized when capabilities are transferred and people from both organizations collaborate. This collaboration relies on the will and ability of managers in both organizations to work together towards the new strategic task. It is critical to replace the "we" versus "they" mentality with a teamwork spirit. The great majority of companies forgo the benefits of an acquisition by either dictating adherence to a predetermined path or avoiding changes in the acquired firm to minimize resistance and disruption.

What you have to do

- **Develop the strategy for cultural integration before the merger.** Decide if you are going to impose one of the cultures, leave them separate, or create a compound culture. Before imposing a culture, be sure that the new culture is better than the one it replaces.

- **Put the leadership team in place quickly.** Minimize uncertainty and a cultural "void." The leadership team must behave as a cohesive group.

- **Perform a thorough cultural assessment.** Understand the differences between the two cultures, identify potential barriers and misunderstandings. Legitimize and discuss the differences. Include organizational systems such as HR, reporting, and IT in this assessment.

- **Decide what you want the new culture to be.** If you are creating a compound culture, define what you want the new culture to be and why. Actively encourage the emergence of something entirely new which builds on the strengths of both partners.

- **Build links between the two organizations.** There is nothing like working together to build understanding.

- **Anchor the new culture through a cultural currency.** Set up a system of incentives and penalties to enforce and encourage the new norms and processes. Make sure the new leadership team acts as role models to continually reinforce the desired behavior. Deal firmly with people who try to undermine the new direction.

- **Have patience.** It takes time for people to adjust to a new cultural reality.

RULE 6

Communication

The real force behind buy-in, orientation, and expectations

Summary

The achievement of merger integration goals depends on how well managers can persuade constituencies to believe in a vision and act to bring it about. This is ultimately a communications task, pure and simple. At first glance, it appears to be the easiest and least complicated aspect of merger integration. But communication won't just happen. Managers must take control of it, plan it carefully, then back it with investment and commitment.

Effective communication requires working out communications goals, pursuing them flexibly, and obtaining feedback to know if they have been achieved. Nonetheless, inadequate communication seems to be common in merger integration.

✳ **Fact one: almost all companies admit their communication is inadequate.**
86 percent of companies said that they failed to communicate their new alliance sufficiently in their merger integration phase.

✳ **Fact two: lack of commitment is the biggest barrier to integration.**
The most-commonly cited barrier to merger integration is "failure to achieve employee commitment." Some 37 percent of respondents cited this as the primary obstacle to overcome, well ahead of obstructive behavior and cultural barriers.

The ultimate communications goal is to have the new company working seamlessly to realize the value of the merger. Viewing communication from this perspective will encourage the level of commitment required to achieve buy-in, provide proper direction and orientation, and properly manage expectations.

You take the TV remote control in your hand and switch on your 24-hour cable news service. The afternoon business program begins, and on the ticker at the bottom of the screen you see the announcement of your merger streaming across.

Your deal is the lead story of the day. The correspondent explains the details almost exactly as they were written in the press release: there is a message of growth, expansion, blazing new trails in new markets. Your own stock price is even moving higher, and the deal is sending a positive shock wave through all global markets.

This situation cannot help but generate a feeling of pride. After all, you and your team have worked day and night for months now to dot every "i" and cross every "t" to make sure this multi-billion dollar deal has the best chance of working. You have a one business vision in place and a management team ready to pursue it. You have prepared yourself to make some growth-oriented moves to send the proper signals to shareholders and the market and to divert attention away from any factory closings or headcount reductions you might need to make. Your transitional team to monitor cultural changes is also in place.

As you are reaching for the champagne, your computer peeps. An e-mail has arrived – urgent priority.

It is an invitation. You have been asked to discuss the merger face-to-face with employee representatives of the company you just acquired. An informal initial meeting, just to let them know where you are headed with this merger. And also, of course, to tell them why you did the deal and what it means for them.

Suddenly it hits you. These are not necessarily the people who watch the 24-hour cable news stations. What have they already heard? Who told them? What in the world are they going to ask you?

And you thought the communication work was over the moment you signed off on that first press release.

T his scenario strikes fear into many CEOs and board members. The most common cause of this fear is the strongly-held perception that communication is a form of subtle and sophisticated, psychological rocket science that a CEO is neither prepared nor willing to take on. But top management is reluctant to communicate openly with new employees for several reasons beyond just simple fear. Top managers feel that they cannot anticipate questions, that they do not have enough clear answers, or that they simply do not want to handle the burden of relaying bad news of job cuts or site closings.

These perceptions – as we will show – are misperceptions.

Nonetheless, communication remains a leadership issue, not just at the CEO or board level, but at all levels. Leaders essentially do three things: they set direction, they surround themselves with people who can steer their staff to follow that direction, and they commit resources effectively. The first two of these are intimately linked to communication, only underscoring its essential role in guiding the merger integration phase.

> What makes mergers stand out as a particular communications challenge is the complex needs of the different constituencies.

What makes mergers stand out as a particular communications challenge is the complex needs of the different constituencies. This complexity makes it that much harder for the newly-formed company to work out its communications goals. How does the new company persuade people to believe in its new vision? How should managers persuade people to act?

Immediately after a merger there is what some analysts have called a "Noah's Ark" effect: you have two of everything on board. There are at least two sets of top managers, two sets of staff, two sets of suppliers, of customers and often investors. Some mergers will inevitably include government as a critical stakeholder as well. Flexibility in approaching these constituencies is key from the outset. Often the needs of the constituencies conflict with the needs of the corporation.

When two multinational chemical companies merged, for example, the new company employed a rich communications approach to resolve the conflict posed by a constituency's desire to maintain the past and the corporate desire to make the integration proceed as quickly as possible. The staff of the acquired company took great pride in its past achievements. It needed to feel that the acquiring company would value these achievements as well as the way they were accomplished. Yet in line with one of the merger's goals, the new company needed to dismantle large parts of the past and combine the two companies quickly.

Investment in the training of "communications reps" formed one key strand of the communication strategy. These reps listened very effectively to grievances, showed that they were understood and appreciated, conveyed a sense for the past, and helped create a foundation from which the company could move forward. The reps also played a role effectively as corporate counselors, even after the merger integration was complete.

The heavy investment paid off for many reasons. First, it showed – more than symbolically – that the company took people's well-being seriously. The effort supported people's individual needs and won their respect. But perhaps the biggest pay-off was that the extensive network – plus the richness of the dialogue – gave superb first-hand feedback about the progress of the merger goals. In other words, the managers consciously "noticed the response." This network fostered an understanding of how well goals were being attained and provided information which could be used to adapt the communication approach as needed.

Communication might be simple in theory, but it is often done insufficiently in practice. Our survey revealed the following facts.

✳ **Fact one:** almost all companies admit their communication is inadequate.
A startling 86 percent of companies said that they failed to communicate their new alliance sufficiently in their merger integration phase.

✳ **Fact two:** lack of commitment is the biggest barrier to integration.
The most-commonly cited barrier to post-merger integration is "failure to achieve employee commitment." Some 37 percent of respondents cited this as the primary obstacle to overcome, well ahead of obstructive behavior and cultural barriers. This lack of commitment, as well as the other barriers shown in Fig. 9, could all fall under the heading "Effects of Insufficient Communication". They emphasize that obtaining buy-in, providing orientation, and managing expectations lie at the core of merger integration.

Why do companies often fall short of their communications goals? There are several reasons involving issues such as leadership, planning, and the commitment of resources.

Some companies are less successful because managers do not take strong enough responsibility. After all, communications departments do exist, which means that some managers feel, even unconsciously, that communication will take care of itself. But it won't. Managers spend so much time ironing out merger details and thinking the big picture through that they begin to take the merger and its underlying rationale for granted. They not only know the details of the merger, but they have the insight, background information, and experience to understand it.

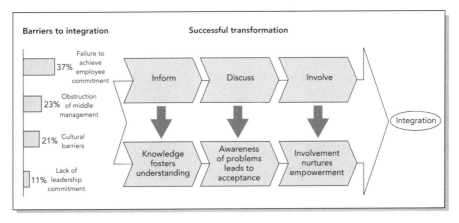

Fig. 9 Lack of employee commitment is the biggest barrier to integration

But the most important stakeholders and the people who will deliver the value from the merger, the rank and file, are months behind the top managers in their thinking. They lack the same insight, background or experience. What they are guaranteed to have is uncertainty and questions. Leaders have an obligation to their stakeholders to start to give the answers, and invest in the networks which will help them to frame new, more helpful questions that they begin to answer for themselves, such as: "How can I prosper in the new environment?"

Sometimes managers are unaware that "non-communication" – or under communication, or thoughtless communication – sends messages as well. The difference is that the sender is not in control of what the messages are. In those cases, the grapevine will ultimately decide. *"They never speak to us"* becomes *"they don't care about us;"* *"they don't understand us"* turns into *"they think we're stupid;"* *"they're going to get rid of us"* becomes *"we think they're stupid;"* and *"I don't trust them"* is turned into *"I'm not going to co-operate."*

The grapevine is the single most effective communications medium in your company. You don't need to assign a merger integration team to establish it. It has no budget. Nobody requires grapevine training, and nobody spends time crafting the slides for it. But it nonetheless works superbly. Constantly feeding the grapevine with positive messages will help sustain and nurture merger integration goals.

> The grapevine is the single most effective communications medium in your company.

When companies fall short of their communications goals, underinvestment is another likely cause. Proper communication requires the proper resources. This work needs full-time support. The existing communication infrastructure, for instance, might be too externally oriented (eg on PR) to handle the internal communication challenges. This leaves companies to rely exclusively on staff in internal departments, including legal, investor relations, marketing, finance and human resources. These people often lack the expertise or the time to focus on internal communication. In some cases, naming a communications director – even someone from outside the organization – can ensure that the communication issues are handled as professionally as possible.

Or maybe communications fail during mergers because communicating effectively with so many constituencies is just so intricate. Clearly, it needs a framework and it needs a plan.

Understand the needs of your target audience

The circumstances in many mergers and acquisitions are quite complex. One of the most delicate situations arises when bitter rivals merge. Regardless of whether the deal was done for offensive or defensive purposes, it remains extremely difficult to suddenly sit down with your former "enemies" and work alongside them. A whole generation of current managers has grown up with Sun Tzu's *The Art of War* and Carl von Clausewitz's *Vom Kriege* as unofficial required reading. Their approach has often filtered down to the lowest staffing levels. It is naïve to think that you can walk in one morning, say that the Iron Curtain in our industry has suddenly fallen overnight, and now we all need to be friends.

Rivalries in businesses often run so deep that companies have a fundamentally low regard for the quality of their rival's products. In the case that the rival is recognized as a quality leader, that company may be viewed as arrogant, aloof, dominating, or intimidating. Over time, these prejudices become so institutionalized that much care is required to break down and remove them.

Overcoming problems like this begins with the construction of an overall framework, as shown in Fig. 10.

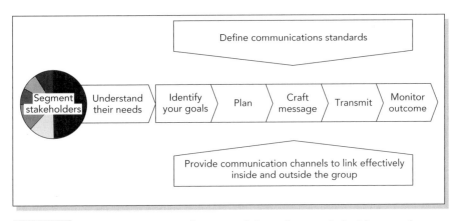

Fig. 10 A communications framework based on stakeholder needs

One of the questions of the staff of an acquired company will certainly be "what does it mean to me?" The following case shows how half the truth can be worse than nothing at all.

Roche/Boehringer Mannheim

Managing a whole package of job cuts and factory closures presents a special communications challenge. An effective goal in these circumstances is to complete these steps as quickly as possible, eliminating any uncertainty that the staff may have, even if that means bad news. This needs courage and clarity. Left to itself, uncertainty will grow with every new day and with every half-fact or incomplete piece of information which the stakeholders receive, regardless of the source.

The integration of Germany's Boehringer Mannheim into the Swiss pharmaceuticals group Roche was hampered by slow or inadequate communication to Boehringer staff. After the deal had been officially announced in May 1997, the 18,000 Boehringer employees waited and wondered about their future.

In October 1997, Roche management announced that there would be a reduction of 5,000 jobs throughout the company. No information, however, was released as to which locations would be affected. Amid this half-the-story approach, many in the workforce imagined the worst case, which slowed down the progress of the merger integration. Roche ultimately needed to invest considerable time and effort to change the employees' perception and develop a relationship based on mutual confidence.

Roche continues to show growth in profit. Despite an anticipated drag on profits due to the Boehringer acquisition, net profit still managed to rise by 3 percent in 1998.

Roche can be found at **www.roche.com**

You have to know your own communications goal

The main reason managers need to understand the needs of constituencies is to help better frame their communications goals in merger integration. The goal is acceptance of specific ideas which either persuade constituencies to buy into the vision or persuade them to act. Knowing your audience allows you to spin the message successfully. The goals can involve putting a broad and diverse group of constituencies at ease, as the case of the merger between South Africa's Anglo-American and Luxembourg's Minorco SA shows. Achieving their goals can make the most sophisticated communications plan necessary.

Anglo plc

The worldwide metals and mining industry has a tradition of cross-holdings and joint ventures as well as billion-dollar merger deals. But few may need to be handled with more sensitivity than the planned merger between South African metals giant Anglo-American and Luxembourg-based mining Minorco SA.

These companies are important to the African economy on a macro-economic scale. Anglo plc, the resulting company, is now listed on the London Stock Exchange at a market capitalization of $10 billion, qualifying it for entry into the FTSE-100 Index. The South African diamond giant De Beers is expected to hold a 40 percent stake in the company.

The deal is designed to rein in two companies which diversified into everything from beer to fertilizer and focus them entirely on growing and exploiting their large portfolio of mining interests. These stretch from coal to gold and cover most of the globe.

The communication challenges arise in part from the listing in London and the shift of focus to a global-oriented UK operation instead of a South African operation. Anglo's history is intimately linked to South Africa's own political and economic situation in this century. Union officials felt that its departure might be interpreted as a blow to the spirit of government established by Nelson Mandela and a sign that South Africa is unable to hold onto its corporate jewels.

Anticipating these concerns, the merger announcement noted up-front that Anglo will remain committed to developing both new and existing interests, not just in South Africa but across the entire continent. This would include social as well as economic investment. The merger parties – assuming they gain approval – would then need to back this paper commitment with tangible "early wins" in order to help smooth the merger integration process.

Anglo plc can be found at **www.angloamerican.co.uk.com**

Develop a plan comprising targets, goals, content, and media

Mergers and acquisitions have two fundamental effects: they disrupt thousands of relationships, some of them established and nurtured over decades. Many of these relationships will be shaken so badly that they can be repaired only with great difficulty. At the same time, mergers create relationships that never existed before. Whether these new relationships will be perceived as opportunities or threats depends on how actively the company communicates and how well it devotes resources to the problem.

Managing all communications in the merger integration phase demands a comprehensive, centrally-controlled plan. Goals need to be written down, content decided, and resources committed. Feedback must be gathered and follow-through ensured. A starting point is shown in Fig. 11, which describes certain target audiences, what the company's goals are vis-à-vis this audience, and how they will be expressed in terms of content and media. As we will discuss below, these four elements are highly interconnected.

> Managing all communications in the merger intergration phase demands a comprehensive, centrally-controlled plan.

This emphasizes the need to develop a concrete plan after assessing your communication needs. From a timing standpoint, this plan can be broken down by weeks, as the simplified figure below illustrates.

This plan is no more than a blueprint and should not be seen as rigid. It must continually be evaluated to reflect feedback and new information.

In some contexts within a merger it is critical to get the message exactly right. In these cases, employ professionals and keep tight control. Any sensitive information needs tight control and a scripted, consistent, unwavering party line. It is no coincidence that in

> When it comes to delivery, the exact words play a crucial role.

the last UK general election, the new Labour Party of current Prime Minister Tony Blair was re-elected on the back of one of the most tightly controlled communications campaigns seen in British politics.

When it comes to delivery, the exact words play a crucial role. The more the communications goal is geared toward bringing action about,

Structure of a basic communications plan			
Target audience	**Goals**	**Content**	**Medium**
Top managers in both companies	Engage their ambition Set up future communications	Merger objectives Merger approach Future potential Earn out bonus scheme Consultation plans	Cascade meetings supported by video Q&A Series of lunch meetings CEO confidential meetings
Project team leaders	Engage their ambition Ensure they understand how to play their role	Merger objectives Merger approach Future potential Individual team goals Team member selection critieria	2-day meetings led by CEO
Staff	Ensure they know the basic merger goals Start constructive discussion Set up lines for future communications	Merger objectives Merger approach Future potential Consultation plans	Cascade meetings led by manager supported by video Q&A Encourage use of confidential e-mail address
Investors	Secure buy recommendation from analysts	Merger objectives Merger approach Future potential	City briefing and reception
Etc			
Source: A.T.Kearney			

Fig. 11 A starting point for a communications plan

the more precise the language needs to be. Furthermore, positive and forward-looking statements help to ensure that doubts and uncertainty are much less likely to arise or grow. The following two simple statements show the difference.

"There will be no staff reductions."

"We all have important roles to play in the future."

Both statements describe the same scenario, but the first sentence raises the very issue the communicator wishes to avoid, simply by using the phrase "staff reduction." In contrast, the second sentence conveys the same fact and the proper sentiment, while making the issue of staff reductions implicit.

In terms of media, the last ten years alone have left managers with a bewildering and continually changing choice of means through which to

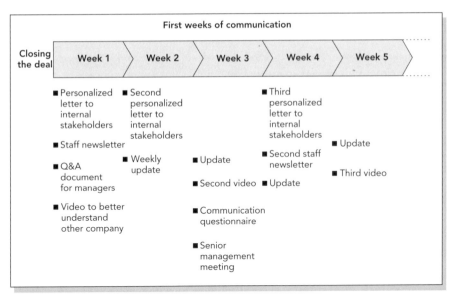

Fig. 12 Starting point for communications timing

communicate. The temptation is to begin a communications plan by listing all of the different media and planning what message to put through them. The often unsatisfying result is a hodgepodge of newsletters, videos, road shows, posters, press releases, e-mails, voicemails, etc, some of which may have no clear purpose. A simple framework can serve as a guide to selecting the proper media. In short, the richness of the medium should match the complexity of the message.

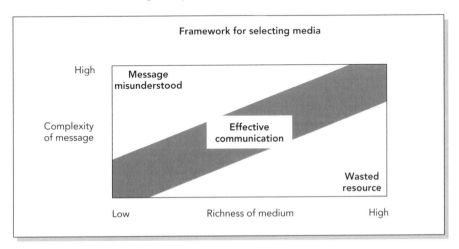

Fig. 13 Matching messages and media essential to effective communication

This tells you that complex messages need a rich medium, ie one that permits or even encourages exploration, questioning, two-way exchange, listening, and feedback. An example of a mismatch would be the communication of the merged company's new set of values on a printed flier. The following example shows how a set of rich media can facilitate the communication and imprinting of important information such as a net set of values.

An international aerospace group was faced with a changing marketplace and increasing competitive pressure. Internally, the risk-averse organization needed to change in order to move quickly and confidently to absorb the companies the group had recently acquired. To bring across the new strategy and communicate the organizational improvements, the group planned a series of communication events based on a workshop format, a rich medium. In detail, the group:

- conducted more than 1,000 one-day workshops with about 20 participants each over three months; these were led by line staff trained to serve as workshop leaders;

- prepared materials in advance, including video feedback from customers;

- engaged employees in dialogue about the situation;

- discussed what behavior would generate the right results.

Senior managers attended every workshop to listen to the groups' own summaries and take questions. The investment came to more than $1 million, but the communications goal was achieved. A greater sense of urgency took root throughout the company, as did a new sense of commitment to the corporate goals.

Monitor the outcome of your communication and act accordingly

Information can become quite distorted as it circulates. Obtaining frequent feedback is therefore essential to determine whether the right message has reached the right people at the right time. The case of Pharmacia & Upjohn illustrates the importance of using feedback to adjust communications goals and judge their success.

Pharmacia & Upjohn

CEO Fred Hassan knew that obtaining feedback would support his recent efforts to bring out the growth possibilities in Pharmacia & Upjohn. He chose a rich medium to support his messages and he built in feedback to his communications. Rather than writing memos, devising some key messages, and stuffing them in the channels, Hassan went on the road and listened more than he spoke.

Through face-to-face meetings, Hassan was not only able to get his points across but also get input and feedback which were built into the plans he launched successfully soon after. His example is simple and worth emulating. He not only understood how well his message was received, but adapted his plans to take account of what he was hearing.

Pharmacia & Upjohn can be found at **www.phu.com**

Impersonal or indirect feedback is equally important. Has the share price gone up? Has the department of trade asked you for a meeting? Has absenteeism gone up? Is the leadership team behaving as it needs to?

The "branding" of communications can have a powerful effect as well. Opportunities to brand are especially abundant when the newly-merged organization adopts an entirely new name such as Novartis, Aventis or Invensys. In the same way that commercial brands stand for much more than the present tag line, consistent use of the same type of platform, the same slogan, and the same design can start to define much more than the immediate message. Everything about the branding should be consistent with the ultimate goal, however, which is making sure that the merged companies work smoothly to create the value that initiated the merger.

The final part of the framework concerns managers' access to staff, customers and other parties with a vested interest. This may vary from deepening personal links to decision makers in government, to providing effective e-mail or voicemail access across the merged group, to providing Internet access to customers. One innovative example of the use of new media to aid communication efforts in the merger integration phase is the Internet. While most companies involved in mega-mergers have a home page, the practice of exploiting this medium to its fullest has yet to become widespread. One exception is the US-based financial services group Wells Fargo, during the planning phase for a merger with Norwest Corporation. The company's website has click-through options to pages dedicated solely to the details of the merger, the latest updates, a list of frequently asked questions, and pages customized for customers, investors and press. It can be found at **www.wellsfargo.com/merger**

You must also honestly assess yourself as a communicator

No matter what people might claim about Winston Churchill or Ronald Reagan, nobody is a born communicator. We are not, however, referring to basic rhetorical skills or the ability to coin a memorable phrase. Rather, we are talking about the commitment to communication.

It might sound trite to phrase it in this manner, but the first step is believing wholeheartedly that the vision you have developed and the strategy you have mapped out to pursue it are sound. Test this by asking yourself a few questions.

- Is your articulation of your vision and your strategic intent clear, compact, and convincing?

- Do you trust yourself to initiate a conversation on your merger and your strategic intent?

- Could you see yourself attending 100 events in one year – with all imaginable stakeholders – to promote the merger and explain its rationale?

If the answer to any of these questions – and especially the first one – is "no," then you are looking at a merger whose failure risk may be too large. As a top manager, your message wields the most power, which means it can bring about the greatest positive effects, or it can do the most damage. You need to be sure yourself of what you are buying into – and that your buy-in is total – before you begin asking others to jump on the bandwagon.

Roger Penske's moves at Detroit Diesel in 1988 showed that his ability to identify and realize early wins was not the only factor which helped him quickly gain buy-in from the company's rank and file. His communication style also served him well.

Detroit Diesel

When Roger Penske invested $300 million for his initial 60 percent stake in Detroit Diesel, he wasted no time in addressing the concerns of the workforce, which feared that job reductions might be coming.

On a Saturday afternoon, at a sports facility near the company's plant, Penske convened a meeting which hundreds of hourly staff attended. He spent the afternoon fielding and answering questions and continually provided reassurance to calm fears of mass layoffs. The meeting was considered so much of a success that he began meeting union leaders on a regular basis and continued to meet with employees to keep them focused on the company's business issues.

The resulting buy-in has helped Penske enforce discipline within the workforce. Their new commitment, aided in part by early wins such as the new cafeteria and the institution of a profit-sharing scheme, manifested itself in hard numbers. Absenteeism fell by half, and productivity rose sufficiently to boost the company's market share eight-fold in just three years.

Detroit Diesel can be found at **www.detroitdiesel.com**

> **The new rule** is to plan your communication according to timing and target, get the word out, and actively obtain feedback.

This means that you do not need to have all the answers, nor feel obligated to fabricate an answer to every question or to improvise when an unanticipated question comes your way. The credibility gained by expressing your commitment through a consistent, firm, and honest approach is crucial over the long term to gaining people's support for the changes required to make the merger work.

What you have to do

- **Recognize that all of your merger goals depend on communication.** You have to persuade other people to believe in your vision and to act to bring it about. This is a communication task, pure and simple.

- **Know your communication goals.** At all times, with all stakeholders, be consciously aware of your own goal for the communication. This also involves knowing your constituencies, including employees, unions, investors, customers, suppliers, the financial community, the local community, and local and national governments.

- **Be flexible.** Use all of your skills to make the best choices about how to communicate most effectively. Use more than one medium and be prepared to change how you communicate whenever necessary.

- **Listen.** Use whatever method you can to understand whether you have achieved your communications goals. Dialogue is the richest form of feedback, but it is certainly not the only one. Indirect indicators such as personal behavior, levels of absenteeism – and, of course, the share price – also tell you how your message has been heard.

- **Remember that you are always communicating.** "Non-communication" is still communication because it sends messages. You're just not in control of what the messages are, and the grapevine will decide. The grapevine is the single most effective communications medium in your company. Give it good reasons to circulate positive messages.

- **Follow a framework to help you manage the complexity.** Understand all your stakeholders, know your own communications goals, write a plan, craft messages positively and effectively, pick appropriate media. Then actively obtain feedback to know when you have achieved your goals. Set high standards and make sure you have channels of access.

- **Check your commitment to your message** and your ability to communicate it consistently, firmly, and honestly.

Risk management

Be proactive, not reactive

Summary

Ask many people to give you a word when you say "risk" and a frequent answer will be "avoid." Risk bears a strongly negative or foreboding connotation in many people's minds. The high returns and strong growth promised by a merger, however, come with comparably strong risks attached.

Without a way to recognize and embrace these risks instead of ducking them, the chances of achieving the high returns your merger promises will be reduced. Fortunately, our survey of 115 transactions around the world showed some encouraging signs that companies are making efforts to proactively face their risks.

✳ **Fact one: proactive risk management is being pursued.**
Some 32 percent of merging companies surveyed already actively pursue formal risk management.

✳ **Fact two: proper risk management can lead to early wins.**
Some of these companies employ risk management so effectively that it has become a source for both early wins and long-term growth.

The downside, of course, is that two-thirds of all companies apparently pursue their post-merger integration without the benefit of a risk management process. The extent and complexity of risk will grow, however, in proportion with the opportunities which large deals create.

When the merger between you and your partner closes today, the greatest managerial risk of your career begins in earnest. A combination of a clear and realistic vision, decisive leadership, and your team's superb and thorough due diligence work gives you a reasonably secure feeling that this is going to work.

On the flight to the first major press conference, you take one last look at your speech, then decide to repeat a brainstorming exercise you did right as the merger negotiations began. You take out a blank legal pad and make two columns. Over the left one you write "Huge opportunities" and over the right one – for lack of a better title – you write "Don't be surprised if…"

As the plane begins its descent, you stop writing and notice something that gives you a bit of apprehension about today's press conference. The first time you did the brainstorming, the list under "Huge opportunities" was twice as long as the "Don't be surprised if…" side. This time the ratio is 3-to-1, and it's in favor of "Don't be surprised if…"

The huge opportunities in the left-hand column are the make-or-break for this merger. If you cannot achieve them, there is no point for the merger and no reason to proceed.

You meet your counterpart CEO shortly before the press conference. He asks why you look so serious. You show your list, which now covers four pages, and point to the right-hand column.

"When this is over today, we'd better get ready, my friend," you say. "We have a lot of work to do."

One motive for writing this book on post-merger integration was not to discourage you from undertaking a merger or acquisition. In fact, it was just the opposite. The willingness to take such billion-dollar risks is fundamental to unlocking growth opportunities, unleashing creative capacity, and – in the end – creating a lot of value. The key is to find ways to manage the risks involved, and not to avoid them.

Steps such as developing a clear, pathbreaking vision, naming management quickly, focusing on growth, and shooting for early wins are all ways to improve your chances for success. But effective and disciplined risk management is one of the key contributing factors to the successful execution of your merger.

One merger that shows that risk-taking is fundamental to growth is the 1998 merger of British Petroleum and Amoco. This deal – much like the even larger union between US oil giants Exxon and Mobil – is fascinating from a historical standpoint, because they both bring parts of the Standard Oil empire back together again. The oil industry thus begins to come full circle after a fragmentation which began when US anti-trust authorities broke up the original Standard Oil in 1911.

BP Amoco

When this $48 billion merger was announced, the trained eyes of analysts and market observers across the globe focused on the estimated $2 billion in synergies and cost savings that the deal promised. If you look deeper, however, you see the growth story which is the real key to making the merger a success. And that growth is intimately linked to risk.

Amoco President Bill Lowrie noted, for example, that there were huge risks for his company in the former Soviet Union, and Amoco might not have had the critical mass to take them on. The link with BP means that the bigger company might be willing and able to take on those challenges. Some of Amoco's other costly and risky projects, for example in Trinidad and Egypt, will also be more manageable.

BP Chief Executive Sir John Browne, who heads the combined company, helped build his reputation within BP by developing innovative ways to navigate financial risk. He and BP Deputy Chief Executive Rodney Chase summed up the chances for the combined company as follows: we can take decisions on a bigger scale, with greater confidence, especially with exploration, because we have more capacity to take risks to create wealth.

BP Amoco can be found at **www.bpamoco.com**

BP Amoco is willing to take risks instead of avoiding them. But willingness alone is not adequate to make sure that risk-taking will lead to the promised wealth and high returns. Companies which merge must know how to put a risk management infrastructure in place to allow them to capitalize on their opportunities and avoid being sidetracked or sideswiped by "the unexpected."

Don't be surprised if ...

- Market analysts do not like your merger plans and recommend "sell."

- Large US pension funds don't like your new board and want to challenge it.

- A subsidiary of the company you just acquired competes against one of your key suppliers.

- A key account manager leaves the company unexpectedly.

- Parties in a product liability suit suddenly begin pushing for a trial.

- The European Commission or the US authorities challenge your merger on anti-trust grounds, as does the country of Australia and the regulatory commission of the US State of Virginia.

- Environmental liabilities such as emissions data or Superfund exposure might increase.

The success of your merger plans hinges on many factors you might have been unaware of at the time of the transaction. But if your comprehensive business due diligence lived up to its name, you have a good head start in identifying the risks on the list above, which is a tiny sample of all the things which can – and often do – go wrong.

Don't avoid risk, embrace it

The traditional rule on risk management says that a company that has just merged should be prepared for unforeseen setbacks, unexpected developments, and unforeseen problems. Nothing will go as planned, so be prepared to react, according to the conventional wisdom.

But in today's world, the circumstances are different. The very nature of competition in global markets is being changed beyond recognition by "unforeseen setbacks, developments, and unforeseen problems." Companies merging today who want to take advantage of future growth opportunities need to recognize that the pace of these developments is increasing. They present risks that require formal management which goes beyond simple preparation.

We find it encouraging and refreshing that many of the companies we examined in our survey are not taking a look at this swirling maelstrom of change and then immediately running for cover. Nor are they foolishly jumping in head first and hoping to swim with the tide for as long as they can. Instead, they are getting a grip on their corner of the world, putting a map together, and confronting the maelstrom. In other words, they are confronting their risks and turning them into opportunities.

✳ **Fact one: proactive risk management is being pursued.**
  Some 32 percent of merging companies in our global survey of 115 transactions already actively pursue formal risk management.

✳ **Fact two: proper risk management can lead to early wins.**
  Some of these companies employ risk management so effectively that is has become a source for both early wins and long-term growth.

The biggest misperception regarding risk management is that it is a form of black magic beyond the comprehension of the mortals who manage merging companies. After all, nobody receives a crystal ball when they graduate from business school. Our only remark on this misperception is simple: get over it.

> The work involved in the creation and use of a risk management infrastructure takes time, attention, and resources.

The work involved in the creation and use of a risk management infrastructure takes time, attention, and resources. It is detail-intensive and it requires considerable momentum. But it is also do-able, and it has many hands-on uses, as shown in Fig. 14.

In the special case of a merger, unique challenges are created and day-to-day ones become more intense and urgent. You have *stakeholder risks*,

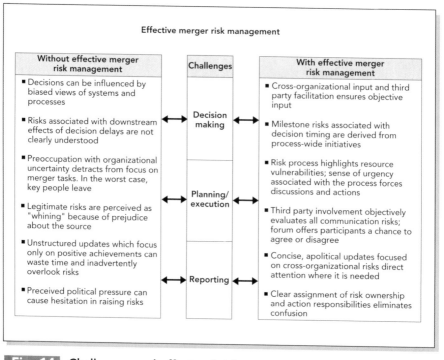

Fig. 14 Challenges and effects of risk management

which could cover everything from the loss of investor confidence, to the loss of key employees, to the loss of key customers. Then there is *execution risk*, which addresses areas such as information technology, the ability to complete projects on time, and the ability to meet other milestones in terms of performance and timing.

Finally there are risks to the very *benefits* promised by the merger. Can your various brands be consolidated or repositioned? Can you consolidate or combine functions to make your operation more efficient and less costly?

You certainly have ambitious plans to meet cost reduction targets. Will they succeed? The integration of you and your merger partner might cause some disruption to customer service. How effective will you be in minimizing this? The integration of your IT systems could hit some bumps. Are you prepared? Your legal reporting requirements have changed in the wake of the acquisition. Are you keeping up?

These are just a few examples of the myriad areas where you have projects and also potential problems. Few mergers reach a stable point and begin their all-out pursuit of growth without making changes in IT and service, or without taking cost out of the business. You certainly will have project teams working on these areas.

Prioritizing your projects is the first step

As we have said in many sections so far, the first step toward success is an assessment. This demands that you have an honest, objective and incisive view of your situation and the obstacles you are facing.

The number of projects required in a post-merger integration varies greatly from merger to merger. The case below illustrates just how many teams might be named to handle various integration projects. For complex mega-mergers, a project total numbering in the hundreds is not unusual.

> The first step towards success is an assessment. This demands that you have an honest, objective and incisive view of your situation and the obstacles you are facing.

SmithKline Beckman and Beecham

The $16.1 billion transatlantic merger between the US-based SmithKline Beckman and UK-based Beecham Group had a head start in its integration. Top management had already co-operated for nine months and used this time to work out many technical, financial and legal issues and to develop a joint business plan.

During the post-merger integration, the combined company tackled a wide range of complex issues by engaging some 2,500 managers as spearheaders from 60 countries working in 300 project teams. This full-scale implementation effort brought individual differences in top management to light, and in the first full year the company's profit came in some $112 million below forecast.

Following some management departures, a sweeping, long-term change management program was implemented throughout the organization. In 1998 earnings per share rose by 10 percent, while sales climbed to around $13 billion. The company's shares have also consistently outperformed the Standard and Poor's 500 over the last five years.

SmithKline Beecham can be found at **www.sb.com**

Prioritizing these projects involves rating them in two areas. The first area is business criticality. Not all projects will have the same effect on your operations, which means you should not lump them all into one large basket.

A project with low business criticality could mean, for example, that the gains from the project would be incremental and the current proc'

– if left in place – would still be sufficient for the time being. A highly-critical project, on the other hand, will have a major impact on the course of your merger. Its completion will be essential for you to maintain a competitive advantage or simply to keep the business operating.

The second scale is complexity. The net complexity of a project is a function of the knowledge and other resources you can bring together on the project, and the magnitude of work to be accomplished, and the level of detail involved. In this case, a low-level project can be managed with a low commitment of resources. A very complex project, in contrast, not only demands a high level of resource commitment, but perhaps a more complicated one. Cross-functional teams, for example, might need to be built, supported, and sustained to make sure that the project is completed in a timely and proper fashion.

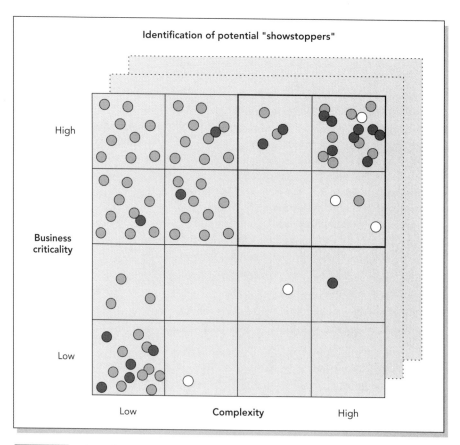

Fig. 15 Identifying the showstoppers

One crucial step in this phase is to make sure that the projects are defined and explained in terminology and language which is understood by all parties. Distortions can easily arise when someone makes an assessment of business criticality or project complexity before they have the same understanding of the tasks involved that their colleagues have.

The results of this work are plotted in a matrix, which gives you your first indication of what priorities you face in your post-merger integration. It provides you with the insights and the sense of urgency regarding what you need to accomplish. The next step is to identify the actual risks involved in the projects, based on priority as shown in the matrix you just developed.

Identify issues, make assumptions, and identify risks

Identifying the risks inherent in your highest priority projects is not a simple matter of brainstorming, fingerpointing and drawing from your previous experience. The first step in assessing the risk in each project is to develop issues, which are nothing more than open questions regarding the project. More than just an exercise in list-making, the development of issues relies on the ability of you and your team to define the key variables or drivers related to each project, to take a broad and – above all – apolitical

> The first step in assessing the risk in each project is to develop issues, which are nothing more than open questions regarding the project.

and objective look at them. You will need to challenge yourself to come up with an exhaustive set.

Once your issues have been defined and agreed upon, you can begin making assumptions about these issues. Again, this demands objectivity and sensitivity. Many of the assumptions you and your team make and agree upon can resolve a great number of the issues and open questions. Some, however, will not bring consensus agreement. They will be open to debate, hard to support, and perhaps based more on conjecture and feeling than solid facts.

Out of this latter group of assumptions – the ones with doubt written all over them – come the risks that you are up against. These risks, as well as their underlying assumptions and related issues, must be included in the project plans.

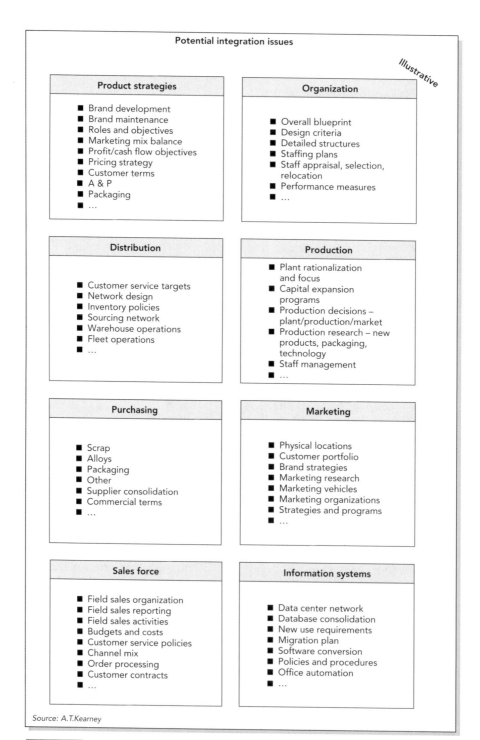

Fig. 16 A small sample of PMI issues

Boeing and McDonnell Douglas

Probably nothing in the world is a better example of a million-dollar thing with lots of 5 cents parts than an airplane. A 747 jetliner, for example, has around 6 million parts, half of which are only fasteners.

One would expect Boeing to be adept at handling complex projects. Its work on integrating the defense business of Rockwell International, for instance, demonstrated how effectively post-merger integration can move forward when it is handled with sensitivity, discipline, and communication skills.

The problem Boeing faced is that the integration of Rockwell was still in progress when it decided to buy struggling rival McDonnell Douglas for $13.4 billion in 1997. When the deal was finally consummated, Boeing Chairman Phil Condit remarked offhandedly that the company needed to make around 5,000 decisions in the next six months.

Many of them were crucial to the viability of the business, including where to base defense and aerospace operations, who should fill key management posts, and what product lines would be discontinued.

The sheer mass of these decisions was a major factor behind Boeing's special charge of $876 million in 1997, which led the company to post a loss for the year of $178 million. The profit situation has since improved, as in 1998 the company earned $1.8 billion on sales of around $56 billion.

Like a snake swallowing its meal, it will still take time for Boeing to digest the McDonnell Douglas and Rockwell acquisitions completely and integrate 210,000 employees under a common cause.

Boeing can be found at **www.boeing.com**

The challenges here, while certainly manageable, cross many different levels and demand a high degree of sensitivity and discipline. You have to balance your striving for a complete set of issues with the demands created by project urgency. You should give the details their due and you should not forget that the contraption which costs $1 million is often brought down by the part which costs 5 cents. But you should not lose your perspective by drilling too deep for too long in a quest for a perfect solution instead of an optimal one.

Categorize your risks by urgency

Risks, like the projects you prioritized in the first step, come in different intensities and have different impacts. They can be classified and then engaged. In contrast to project prioritization, however, the categorization is one-dimensional, straightforward, and understandable. Your risks are classified into high-medium-low.

Urgent risks, as you might expect, are the showstoppers which can damage or even kill everything you have worked on. The effects could range from a legal challenge to your merger, such as a pending and unresolved lawsuit, and environmental impact, or an anti-trust case whose outcome is uncertain. Even with the European Union's newly revised procedures on handling anti-trust cases, under which the European Commission promises a quick decision within four weeks or an ultimate decision in five months, the uncertainty about the outcome can take its toll.

In other cases, you might be facing the loss of a key account or the loss of a customer base in a particular segment. Or you may be facing a cost situation whose impact cannot yet be quantified. Even a positive benefit such as additional capacity can pose a risk when its integration takes longer than anticipated. The case of Southwest Airlines and Morris Air may not have been a mega-merger, but the $134 million deal shows that risk assessment is not the exclusive requirement of complex, multinational mergers.

Southwest Airlines

Southwest purchased Utah-based Morris Air for $134 million in stock in December 1993 and swiftly integrated it into its operation. The airline had developed a post-merger execution plan which resulted from a pre-merger due diligence covering not only financial considerations, but also labor relations, accounting methods, sourcing, and a plane-by-plane review of Morris's asset base.

While the broader due diligence helped facilitate a rapid integration, the magnitude of the integration basically gave Southwest more capacity than it could handle with its current booking and reservation agreements. The Morris purchase resulted in a double-digit increase in the airline's number of available seats, most on routes where Southwest had little or no operating experience. The resulting problems with reservation systems was one of many factors behind the decline in the company's share price, which had fallen by almost 50 percent by February 1995 before recovering all of the lost ground.

Southwest can be found at **www.iflyswa.com**

Risks of moderate urgency still come with burdens and complications, but do not have the potentially lethal quality of the urgent risks. A moderate risk would perhaps have a major cost impact, would be difficult to resolve or work around, or might cause noticeable friction with stake-holders such as customers, investors or employees.

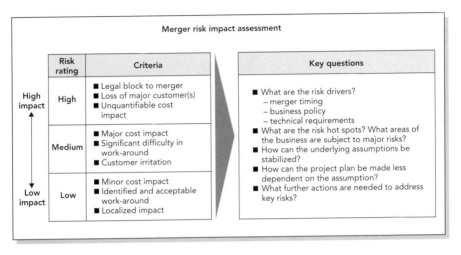

Fig. 17 Merger risk rating by criticality

Less urgent risks – which have the lowest impact on your business – are much more contained. Their worst-case cost impacts are minor, and the required work has been identified and seen as acceptable. These risks often have a localized impact, but much less of an impact in the perspective of the corporation as a whole.

One aspect of risk management is the integration of information technology (IT). In many mergers IT integration is the linchpin of the entire business. Recognizing potential conflicts beforehand is essential in such cases.

Salomon Smith Barney

When the New York-based brokerage Smith Barney Inc planned to merge with Salomon Inc in 1997, Smith Barney's CEO asked his CIO during the pre-merger talks to review the potential IS (information system) compatibilities between the two companies. The goal was to feel confident that the systems could be integrated where appropriate. After a close review of Salomon's systems the CIO could report that there would be no major problems, thanks to similar platforms at the front-end and back office. The merger was negotiated and the two companies could be combined without any showstoppers due to IT.

Salomon Smith Barney can be found at **www.smithbarney.com**

Embrace your risks and then reprioritize

Up to this point you have made considerable progress in making sense out of the project puzzle pieces. You and your team have prioritized them, so that you can begin thinking about proper resource allocation decisions.

You have thought the projects through – based on these priorities – and defined their underlying issues. Drawing on the knowledge, experience and facts you have available, you have made assumptions about these issues, eliminated many, but kept the shakier ones around for further discussion and exploration. In other words, you have identified your risks.

Staying with the systematic approach, you then classified these risks based on their ability to undermine your business. The final step in this cycle is to gain an even deeper understanding of your risks, and then make the decision to resolve them head on or to lower the dependence of your projects on them.

By resolving them, we mean that you take action to overcome them directly. Your specific actions should be designed to address the risks. This means making a proactive decision to seize an opportunity by overcoming the risks and eliminating them by action rather than simply ducking them. Making your projects less sensitive to a particular risk means making the project less dependent on that particular risk or assumption. The step is also conscious and proactive, but the actions involved address risk minimization rather than risk confrontation.

The process of arriving at these action decisions is likewise systematic. You need to ask yourself again what the drivers are behind the risk you are facing. You need to explore precisely what areas of your business will take collateral damage if the risk delivers a big hit to one primary area. You and your team need to assess what information and resources you require to bring your projects onto safer ground.

This is not just theory: it's been done

The type of systematic process described in this section does not gather dust on a chalkboard. It has survived and proven itself in various forms in actual merger situations, where honest and objective assessments of risks were absolutely crucial to making the merger a success.

The situation of every company involved in a mega-merger is ripe for some form of risk management infrastructure. These billion-dollar deals involve tens of thousands of customers, tens of thousands of employees, thousands of line items on the sourcing side, hundreds or thousands of individual product variations, with all of this spread over upwards of 100 countries. Because of both the volume and intricacy of their customer relationships, which are in a constant state of flux, financial institutions are especially aware of the need to implement proper risk management procedures. An illustrative example is the merger between the leading US banks Chase Manhattan and Chemical Bank.

Chase Manhattan and Chemical Bank

Chemical Bank and Chase Manhattan faced many risks when they merged in 1996. The merger needed to be carried out quickly, while keeping the ongoing businesses running. The timely setting of priorities helped the two banks co-ordinate 1,300 individual projects over 20 months.

Project areas covered by the risk management program, including human resources, were unified into one department. Other difficult but high-priority tasks included the reconciliation of the two payment systems (due to their different approaches to bonuses, fringe benefits and social benefits) and the updating, altering, and integrating of information technology systems. The company succeeded in installing 10,000 personal computers and changing more than 1,000 servers in a single, company-wide effort.

Chase's success in its post-merger integration has been reflected in its stock price, which rose to $91 in 1999 from $45 in 1996.

Chase can be found at **www.chase.com**

In merger situations – which are always characterized by uncertainty, anxiety, cultural differences, as well as internal and external politics – the risk management methodology outlined above provides clarity and focus. It encourages your organization to discuss relevant risks and issues in a common language. It provides you with a means to take politics out of the process as much as possible, and to build in objectivity.

The biggest attraction of this methodology, however, lies in its ability to shift your focus from risk avoidance to proactive risk management. By overcoming or minimizing the risks your merged organization faces, you come much closer to capturing the growth opportunities that are expressed in your corporate vision and which drove you and your merger partner to come together in the first place.

The new rule: prioritize projects, then identify, categorize, and embrace risks, and do it continually.

High returns and high risk are inextricably linked. Taking control of your risks is taking control of your future. The coin of merger success and merger failure is flipped in the air the moment your deal is consummated, and this methodology can give you an edge in making sure that this coin lands "success-side-up."

What you have to do

- **Assess your situation,** then prioritize your post-merger integration projects according to their business criticality and their complexity.

- **Derive the risks inherent in your project** by making a thorough examination of the relevant issues, then making assumptions regarding those issues.

- **Categorize your risks** according to "high-medium-low" in order to pinpoint the showstoppers which can spell death to your merger plans.

- **Vigorously attack those risks you can overcome,** and minimize the importance of the ones which are not as easily and quickly overcome.

- **Monitor the process diligently and repeat it** from the beginning on a regular basis. Every move you make changes your internal circumstances, and your external circumstances are constantly changing as well. This is a fluid, dynamic process, not a one-off solution.

PART 3

The future

Merger outlook:
you haven't seen anything yet

T he solid majority of the mergers and acquisitions which took place in 1998 and 1999 – especially the so-called mega mergers – involved at least one company based in the United States or the United Kingdom. Even today, the media in continental Europe occasionally refer to the swiftness, size and severity of mergers and acquisitions as an "Anglo-Saxon" way of doing business. But things are changing. The pace of corporate integration within and beyond the European Union continues to accelerate. M&A activity in Japan has also increased, although the focus remains on domestic deals.

In terms of swiftness, size and severity, many recent transactions have set off alarm bells among labor leaders, anti-trust authorities, and politicians with protectionist leanings. After all, the combined Gross Corporate Product (GCP) of DaimlerChrysler, Exxon Mobil, and Citigroup is rapidly approaching the Gross Domestic Product (GDP) of countries such as Canada, one of the G-7 countries. Suddenly, a world where truly global corporations may soon become more important and influential than nation states does not seem farfetched. Signs have begun to emerge that companies will even assume functions formerly fulfilled by the state, such as health care, education, and life insurance.

> Suddenly, a world where truly global corporations may soon become more important and influential than nation states does not seem farfetched.

"Corporatism" seems to be gaining more tangible day-to-day influence on people's lives than the governments of the world's leading countries. Is this the manifestation of a US political vision which has gone from John F Kennedy's "New Frontier" through George Bush's "New World Order" to Bill Clinton's "It's the Economy, Stupid?"

If you feel that this thinking reflects an almost embarrassing "Western" focus, you are probably correct. In the rush to examine and explore mergers such as DaimlerChrysler and BP Amoco, observers tend to suppress how fragmented and parochial the "global" marketplace still is, even though it has changed radically in the last decade. Saudi Arabia controls the world's largest petroleum company. China plays home to the world's largest cigarette maker, while the largest telephone company is based in Japan. One of the largest natural gas explorers, meanwhile, is Russian-based, as is one of the world's largest producers of non-ferrous metals. Where is the "West?" Even a company on the scale of Exxon Mobil produces only 4 percent of the world's crude oil.

What is true is that the West is changing at the fastest pace as Europe begins to catch up. It is no wonder that Ron Sommer, the Chairman of Deutsche Telekom, fears his company might end up as a regional, second-tier player if it doesn't expand. Even in Japan, cracks in the wall of regulation and tradition are opening the door for foreign companies to make acquisitions.

In other words, consolidation and globalization have barely begun. Mergers like DaimlerChrysler do not mark the end of a process or the crest of a merger wave, but rather the beginning of a merger and acquisitions trend which will be more far-reaching and complex than anything we have encountered thus far. The transactions which will come in the next five to ten years will make today's mega-mergers look like obvious grasps at low-hanging fruit. From a global perspective, the staggering growth synergies and efficiency synergies available have barely been identified, never mind tapped.

> The transactions which will come in the next five to ten years will make today's mega-mergers look like obvious grasps at low-hanging fruit.

This complexity and scope will place even greater demands on the managers in charge of post-merger integration. But as we mentioned in our rule on risk management, we decided to write this book to encourage you to pursue the rewards which mergers and acquisitions can bring. Even more careful and conscious attention to the rules of post-merger integration will make these risks worth taking.

But what can we expect in the next five to ten years, if the pace of consolidation and globalization really begins to gather momentum? What are the scenarios which are likely to emerge in a truly global corporate landscape? We would like to discuss four scenarios which appear quite probable.

Will we have only three players per industry worldwide?

Within the next five to ten years – depending on the industry – consolidation will reach a peak, as will the merger and acquisition activity which will drive it. Beyond that time frame, only smaller acquisitions will occur, as major players augment their product, regional or skill portfolio. What does this mean for you? Be among the first or be left with the leftovers – this is entirely your choice.

> The dawn of the global conglomerate with $1 trillion in annual revenues is inevitable in the short- to medium-term.

The companies which will result from these future transactions will dwarf the deals of the last two years. Despite all the talk of consolidation thus far in the automobile and pharmaceutical industries, even the largest companies are barely able to claim even 10 percent market share on a truly global basis. The simple arithmetic here means that the dawn of the global conglomerate with $1 trillion in annual revenues is inevitable in the short- to medium-term. What current companies will be involved and where these companies will be headquartered is anybody's guess.

One thing, however, is certain. The creation of companies of this scale and scope will not mark the end of the small businesses which have fueled the rise of the US economy in the last decade and form the cultural and corporate backbone of countries like Germany, Italy and Spain. Quite the contrary. This new landscape will provide room for more entrepreneurial local and regional companies which thrive on customer service and individualized products. Although the revenue gap between these companies and the global players will be gigantic – maybe $100 million versus $100 billion – the cleverer and nimbler of these companies will not lack opportunities.

Competition will also be newly-defined. Small entrepreneurial companies can focus regionally on delighting the customer, while the large monoliths can potentially focus globally on cost leadership in the beginning, while at the same time trying to serve smaller market segments cost efficiently. These smaller companies will, in effect, become links in parts of different value chains rather than owning the total value chain. They will be strong competitors of the major players in their respective regions and will remain highly profitable because they do not need to own a large asset base.

When will we see the first truly global mega-merger?

> Instead of the old merger equation of "one plus one is more than two," we will see companies facing the challenge of combining "one plus one plus one" into more than three.

As we mentioned earlier, DaimlerChrysler marks not the end of an era, but rather a watershed. The result of this impending sea change will mean that the continuation of the current merger wave will see more European, American and Asian companies coming together. Instead of the old merger equation of "one plus one is more than two," we will see companies facing the challenge of combining "one plus one plus one" into more than three.

The future will bring more combinations of the top players in the markets. A high level of diversity will raise new cultural issues. Appropriate diversity management skills will become a critical differentiating factor of the future. American companies, having been trained in diversity management for decades, could become acquisition targets for precisely that reason.

This process will inevitably create friction among anti-trust authorities, as oligopolies or even potential monopolies emerge. In anti-trust policy and approval processes, the United States still ranks as a trendsetter, but the European Commission has recently streamlined and clarified its merger approval process as well. On the corporate side, however, speed and professional divestiture of businesses will become more of an issue. This will require tremendous skill to generate adequate value for shareholders, while ensuring that regulatory or anti-trust processes do not drag on forever.

To what degree will mature industries be reshaped? And what is the future of "new" industries?

The meshing of companies from new, entrepreneurial industries and those from traditional or smokestack industries will occur for a variety of reasons, including:

- providing new channels to buy and sell;
- securing entrepreneurial staff to enable companies in older industries to transform themselves;
- re-configuring value chains.

When the focus on core competencies came into vogue, the old adage of "stick to your knitting" underwent a renaissance. But merging only with companies on your home turf will soon become stale. The idea of "more of the same" does not represent an appropriate value proposition for Internet-educated consumers.

Consequently, concentric mergers with the aim of re-designing or re-configuring a traditional value chain will increase in importance. The business leaders of the twenty-first century will be the senior managers who are able to anticipate trends and make the moves which result in the creation of entirely new value chains.

Equity markets will initially be hesitant to reward companies who intend to reconfigure their value chain by acquiring or merging with parts of another one. Investors claim to have learned lessons from previous attempts in this direction – such as AT&T and NCR or Quaker Oats and Snapple.

Will the value of the brand as a point for customer recognition increase tremendously?

Established brands will provide the consumers with a feeling of familiarity and stability in a rapidly changing world. This need or appreciation of familiarity is having a significant impact on the business-to-business world as well. But as global brands spread, the name of a corporation that ultimately controls those brands becomes less important. Consumers are already identifying more with product brands such as Dodge, Mercedes, Tempo, Huggies, and Snickers than with the companies behind those products.

> Consumers are already identifying more with product brands such as Dodge, Mercedes, Tempo, Huggies, and Snickers than with the companies behind those products.

Consequently, the giant players of any industry will try to amass as many brands as possible and will pay large premiums to secure those brands which may hurt their profitability. We have already seen this movement in consumer products and will definitely witness it soon in industrial goods.

What does all this mean for post-merger integration?

The ultimate outcome of most corporate mergers will continue to depend on the success of the merger integration effort. That will not change. What will change are the most accurate measures of such success, given the trend toward growth mergers involving similarly-sized partners.

The pursuit of growth will create winners who distinguish themselves by expertly blending time-tested post-merger integration techniques with new but still unproven techniques. For others, the economies of scale they had hoped for may soon reach a point of diminishing returns: foreign cultures are much more likely to clash; complex product and service lines are in danger of becoming hopelessly entangled; and some household brand names of previous generations will disappear entirely.

Creating a successful merger between two companies used to be a common sense exercise in logistical planning and operational integration. Nowadays this "exercise" has given way to a dynamic and future-oriented process, best orchestrated by corporate leaders who plan to stick around. With greater risks and challenges, of course, comes a greater potential to create global corporations of unprecedented size and import. A company's ability to capitalize on these new opportunities for growth is what will mark it as a global leader.

Index